Holiday Gifts-in-a-Jar Cookbook

A Collection of Holiday Gifts-in-a-Jar Recipes

Gifts-in-a-Jar Cookbook Series – Book 3

Karen Jean Matsko Hood

Holiday Gifts-in-a-Jar Cookbook
A Collection of Holiday Gifts-in-a-Jar Recipes

Gifts-in-a-Jar Cookbook Series – Book 3

Karen Jean Matsko Hood

Published by

Whispering Pine Press International, Inc.
Your Northwest Book Publishing Company

2510 North Pines Road, Suite 206, Sales Room
Spokane Valley, WA 99206-7636 USA
Phone: (509) 928-7888 | Fax: (509) 922-9949
Email: sales@whisperingpinepress.com
Websites: www.WhisperingPinePress.com
www.WhisperingPinePressBookstore.com
Blog: www.WhisperingPinePressBlog.com
SAN 253-200X
Printed in the U.S.A.

Published by Whispering Pine Press International, Inc.
2510 North Pines Road, Suite 206, Sales Room
Spokane Valley, WA 99206-7636 USA

For sales outside the United States, please contact the Whispering Pine Press International, Inc., International Sales Department.

Manufactured in the United States of America. This paper is acid-free and 100% chlorine free.

Book and Cover Design by Artistic Design Service, Inc.
Spokane Valley, WA 99206-7636 USA
www.ArtisticDesignService.com

Library of Congress Control Number (LCCN): 2014908345

Hood, Karen Jean Matsko
Title: Holiday Gifts-in-a-Jar Cookbook, A Collection of Holiday Gifts-in-a-Jar Recipes, Gifts-in-a-Jar Cookbook Series – Book 3

ISBN: 978-1-59649-127-4   case bound
ISBN: 978-1-59649-651-4   perfect bound
ISBN: 978-1-59434-737-5   spiral bound
ISBN: 978-1-59649-957-7   E-PDF
ISBN: 978-1-59210-654-7   E-PUB
ISBN: 978-1-59434-629-3   E-PRC

First Edition: November 2014
1. Cookbook (*Holiday Gifts-in-a-Jar, A Collection of Holiday Gifts-in-a-Jar Recipes, Gifts-in-a-Jar Cookbook Series – Book 3*)

Holiday Gifts-in-a-Jar Cookbook
A Collection of Holiday Gifts-in-a-Jar Recipes
Gifts-in-a-Jar Cookbook Series – Book 3

Gift Inscription

To: _____

From: _____

Date: _____

Special Occasion: _____

Special Message:

_____

_____

_____

_____

_____

_____

**It is always nice to receive a personal note to
create a special memory.**

www.WhisperingPinePress.com
www.WhisperingPinePressBookstore.com

Dedications

To my husband and best friend, Jim.

To our seventeen children: Gabriel, Brianne Kristina and her husband Moulik Vinodkumar Kothari, Marissa Kimberly and her husband Kevin Matthew Franck, Janelle Karina and her husband Paul Joseph Turcotte, Mikayla Karlene, Kyler James, Kelsey Katrina, Corbin Joel, Caleb Jerome, Keisha Kalani Hiwot, Devontay Joshua, Kianna Karielle Selam, Rosy Kiara, Mercedes Katherine, Jasmine Khalia Wengel, Cheyenne Krystal, and Annalise Kaylee Marie.

To Nola Paige, Zoey Karina, and future grandchildren.

To our foster grandchildren: Courtney, Lorenzo, and Leah.

To my brother, Stephen, and his wife, Karen.

To my husband's ten siblings: Gary, Colleen, John, Dan, Mary, Ray, Ann, Teresa, Barbara, Agnes, and their families.

In loving memory of my mom, who passed away in 2007; my dad, who passed away in 1976; and my sister, Sandy, who passed away due to multiple sclerosis in 1999.

To Sandy's three sons: Monte, Bradley, and Derek. To Monte's wife, Sarah, and their children: Liam, Alice, Charlie, and Samuel and their foster children. To Bradley's wife, Shawnda, and their children: Anton, Isaac, and Isabel.

To our foster children past and present: Krystal, Sara, Rebecca, Janice, Devontay Joshua, Mercedes Katherine, Zha'Nell, Makia, Onna, Cheyenne Krystal, Onna Marie, Nevaeh, and Zada, our future foster children, and all foster children everywhere.

To the Court Appointed Special Advocate (CASA) Volunteer Program in the judicial system which benefits abused and neglected children.

To the Literacy Campaign dedicated to promoting literacy throughout the world.

Holiday Gifts-in-a-Jar Cookbook

Table of Contents

Holiday Gifts-in-a-Jar Cookbook
A Collection of Holiday Gifts-in-a-Jar Recipes
Gifts-in-a-Jar Cookbook Series – Book 3

Introduction

Holidays are such an important time for families and friends to create special moments and memories. Homemade gifts are thoughtful ways to let the people in your life know you care about them during the holiday season. The uniqueness of home-made gifts inspired my Gifts-In-A-Jar Cookbook series.

The Gifts-in-a-Jar Cookbook Series would not be complete without *Holiday Gifts-in-a-Jar Cookbook,* because gifts-in-a-jar are popular and easy to make. They can also be made ahead and this can help avoid the last minute stress of shopping for gifts during the busy holiday season.

I hope you enjoy reading it as well as trying out all of the recipes. This cookbook is designed for easy use and is organized into alphabetical sections: beverages, breads, cookies, scones, seasonings, side dishes, and soups.

Do enjoy your holiday reading and recipe planning, but more importantly, have fun with those you care about while you are cooking and preparing gifts. Happy Holiday season from the author Karen Jean Matsko Hood.

Following is a collection of recipes gathered and modified by Karen Jean Matsko Hood.

Holiday Gifts-in-a-Jar Cookbook
A Collection of Holiday Gifts-in-a-Jar Recipes
Gifts-in-a-Jar Cookbook Series – Book 3

Beverages

Table of Contents

Page

Café Bavarian Mint Flavored Coffee Mix-in-a-Jar

Coffee lovers will enjoy this festive chocolate and mint flavored mix.

Ingredients:

- ¼   c. powdered creamer
- ⅓   c. sugar
- ¼   c. instant coffee
- 3   Tbs. powdered baking cocoa
- 3   hard candy peppermints

Directions:

1. Place all ingredients in a blender and process until finely ground.
2. Store by sealing airtight in a glass jar.
3. Spoon in cup by tablespoons according to taste and add hot water.

Directions for Tag

Ingredients:

- 1-2 Tbs. mix, or to taste
       hot water

Directions:

1. Spoon mix into a mug and pour hot water over.
2. Enjoy!

Double Chocolate Peppermint Candy
Hot Cocoa Mix-in-a-Jar

Enjoy this delightful mix after a hectic day of hitting the after-holiday sales. It also makes a hearty treat after a chilly afternoon of sledding, ice skating, or building snow creatures!

Ingredients:

1	c. instant skim milk powder
1	c. unsweetened cocoa powder
1	c. white sugar
½	tsp. salt
½	c. crushed peppermint candy
½	c. mini semisweet chocolate chips

Directions:

1. Add skim milk powder, cocoa powder, sugar, and salt to a food processor. Pulse until thoroughly mixed.
2. Transfer the mix to a large bowl. Add crushed peppermint candy and mini semisweet chocolate chips. Stir until distributed throughout the mixture.
3. Store mixture in an airtight, quart-sized container. Decorate container as desired.

Directions for Tag

Directions:

1. For each serving, place ⅓ cup cocoa mix in a mug and stir in 1 cup boiling water.

French Vanilla Coffee Mix-in-a-Jar

Need a pick-me-up? A cup of French Vanilla Coffee will bring renewed energy.

Ingredients:

- ⅓   c. instant coffee
- 1   c. instant skim milk powder
- ½   c. powdered nondairy coffee creamer
- ⅓   c. white sugar
- ¼   c. French vanilla instant pudding mix

Directions:

1. Add ingredients to a food processor. Pulse until thoroughly mixed and you have a smooth powder.
2. Pack the mix into an airtight pint-sized jar for storage.

Directions for Tag

Directions:

1. For each serving, place ¾ cup of boiling water in a mug and stir in 2 heaping teaspoons of mix.

Hot Chocolate Mix-in-a-Jar

Package this hot chocolate mix in an attractive jar and decorate according to the occasion. This is always a welcome gift to give or to receive.

Ingredients:

- 3   c. powdered milk
- ½   c. unsweetened cocoa powder
- ¾   c. sugar

Directions:

1. Sift ingredients together into a large bowl.
2. Pack the mix into an airtight jar for storage.

Directions for Tag

Ingredients:

- 2-4 Tbs. mix, or to taste
       hot water

Directions:

1. Spoon mix into a mug and pour hot water over.
2. Enjoy!

Spiced Tea Mix-in-a-Jar

This makes a quick and easy mix for gift giving.

Ingredients*:*

9	oz. powdered orange breakfast drink
4	oz. powdered lemon flavored ice tea drink
1½	c. sugar
3	tsp. ground cinnamon
2	tsp. ground cloves
1	tsp. ground ginger

Directions:

1. Blend together orange drink powder, lemon ice tea powder, sugar, and spices in a large jar.
2. Label and store in tightly covered decorated jars at room temperature, no longer than 6 months.

Directions for Tag

1. For each serving mix 3 teaspoons spiced tea mix and 1 cup boiling water together in a mug until mix is dissolved.
2. Garnish each with a twist of lemon or orange peel and a cinnamon stick if desired.

Yields: 5¼ cups mix.

Holiday Gifts-in-a-Jar Cookbook
A Collection of Holiday Gifts-in-a-Jar Recipes
Gifts-in-a-Jar Cookbook Series – Book 3

Breads

Table of Contents

Apple Bread Mix-in-a-Jar

Late summer apples bring wonderful flavor to this gift-in-a-jar that everyone will enjoy.

Ingredients for bread mix:

- ¾ c. sugar
- 1⅓ c. all purpose flour
- ½ tsp. baking powder
- ½ tsp. salt
- 1 tsp. cinnamon

Directions:

1. Measure all ingredients into a bowl then give it a quick stir with a whisk.
2. Pour half the mixture onto a piece of waxed paper.
3. Lift the paper at the corners and pour into a 16 oz. mason jar.
4. Tap jar against the counter to let mixture settle. Then add the rest. Give jar a final tap.

Directions for Tag

Additional Ingredients:

- ½ c. canola oil
- 1 egg
- ½ tsp. vanilla extract
- 1½ c. chopped apples

Directions:

1. Preheat oven to 350 degrees F.
2. In medium bowl, mix oil, eggs, and vanilla with dry ingredients. Then fold apples into the batter (it will be thick).
3. Pour into a loaf pan and bake 45 to 60 minutes.

Apricot Bread Mix-in-a-Jar

Our family loves apricots and this not only makes tasty bread, it is also a lovely gift.

Ingredients for bread mix:

2½ c. quick biscuit mix
½   c. sugar
1   tsp. baking powder
¼   tsp. salt
¾   c. dried apricots, chopped
¾   c. nuts

Directions:

1. Layer in 1-quart wide-mouth (makes it easier to pack down) canning jar in order listed above.
2. After each layer, pack the layer down.

Directions for Tag

Additional Ingredients:

1¼ c. milk
1   tsp. vanilla extract
2   eggs, slightly beaten
½   c. butter, softened

Directions:

1. Preheat oven to 350 degrees F.
2. In large bowl, mix ingredients of the jar together with milk, vanilla, eggs, and butter.
3. Spoon batter into a large loaf pan that is well greased, with waxed paper in the bottom.
4. Bake for 1 hour or until knife inserted in the center comes out clean.

Banana Bread Mix-in-a-Jar

Most people love banana bread and this is a fun treat and present.

Ingredients:

2⅔ c. white sugar
⅔   c. vegetable shortening
4   eggs
⅔   c. buttermilk
1   tsp. vanilla extract
3½ c. white flour
½   tsp. nutmeg
1   tsp. cinnamon
2   tsp. baking soda
1   tsp. baking powder
1   tsp. salt
2   c. mashed, ripe bananas
⅔   c. chopped nuts (optional)

Directions:

1. Preheat oven to 325 degrees F.
2. In large bowl, cream sugar and shortening with electric mixer.
3. Add eggs and mix well.
4. Add buttermilk and vanilla and mix well.
5. Place dry ingredients in separate bowl and mix well.
6. Add creamed ingredients to dry ingredients; mix well.
7. Gently stir in mashed bananas and nuts.
8. Prepare 7 one-pint wide-mouth canning jars with vegetable shortening.
9. Place 1 cup batter in each jar; do not use more than 1 cup or batter will overflow and jar will not seal.
10. Place jars evenly spaced on a baking sheet.

11. Bake 45 minutes or until a toothpick inserted in center comes out clean.
12. Working quickly, wipe rim, place lid and ring on jar and secure. Jars will seal quickly.
13. Repeat with remaining jars.
14. When ready to serve, bread will slide out.

Carrot Raisin Bread Mix-in-a-Jar

This moist carrot cake is delicious. I like to add walnuts to mine, but either way it is good.

Ingredients:

2⅔   c. sugar
⅔   c. shortening
4   eggs
⅔   c. water
2   c. carrots, shredded
3½   c. flour
¼   tsp. ground cloves
1   tsp. cinnamon
1   tsp. baking powder
2   tsp. baking soda
1   tsp. salt
1   c. raisins
¾   c. walnuts, chopped

Directions:

1. Preheat oven to 325 degrees F.
2. Sterilize 6 wide-mouth pint-size canning jars, metal rings, and lids. Don't use any other size jars.
3. Grease inside, but not the rim of jars.
4. In large bowl, cream sugar and shortening; beat in eggs and water; add carrots.
5. In medium bowl, sift together flour, cloves, cinnamon, baking powder, baking soda, and salt; add to batter.
6. Stir in raisins and walnuts.
7. Pour 1 cup of batter into prepared jars. Do not use more than 1 cup or batter will overflow and jar will not seal.
8. Place jars evenly spaced on a baking sheet.
9. Bake 45 minutes.

10. While cakes are baking, bring a saucepan of water to a boil and carefully add jar lids.
11. Remove pan from heat and keep hot until ready to use.
12. Remove jars from oven one at a time keeping remaining jars in oven.
13. Make sure jar rims are clean. If they're not, jars will not seal correctly.
14. Place lids on jars and screw rings on tightly.
15. Jars will seal as they cool.
16. Cakes will slide right out when ready to serve.

Pumpkin Spice Bread Mix-in-a-Jar

Most pumpkin bread pre-sealed in old-fashioned jars makes a welcome treat. With this one recipe you can give away 8 delicious breads.

Ingredients:

8	canning jars, 12-oz.
8	new lids
8	rings
1	c. raisins
2	c. unbleached flour
2	tsp. baking soda
¼	tsp. baking powder
½	tsp. salt
2	tsp. cloves
2	tsp. cinnamon
1	tsp. ginger
4	egg whites, whipped
2	c. granulated sugar
1	c. butter, softened
2	c. pumpkin

Directions:

1. Preheat oven to 325 degrees F.
2. Place a baking sheet onto middle rack and remove top rack from oven.
3. Before starting batter, wash jars, lids, and rings in hot soapy water and let drain, dry, and cool to room temperature.
4. Generously grease inside of jars with butter.
5. In medium bowl, combine raisins, flour, baking soda, baking powder, salt, cloves, cinnamon, and ginger; mix well.
6. In mixing bowl, combine egg whites, sugar, butter, and pumpkin.
7. Add dry ingredients to egg white mixture; mix well.
8. Divide batter among jars (should be slightly less than half full).

9. Carefully wipe rims clean, then place jars on baking sheet (or they'll tip over) in the center of oven.
10. Bake 40 minutes.
11. Keep lids in hot water until they're used.
12. When cakes are done, remove jars which are HOT from oven one at a time.
13. If rims need cleaning, use moistened paper towel.
14. Carefully put lids and rings in place, then screw tops on.
15. Place jars on a wire rack; they will seal as they cool.
16. Once jars are cool, decorate with round pieces of cloth.
17. Unscrew the ring; the lid should be sealed by now.
18. Lace a few cotton balls on top of the lid (gives it a poof on top), then a piece of cloth (about 3 inches larger than the lid) on top and screw the ring back on.

Zucchini Bread Mix-in-a-Jar

This is a great gift to make for summer treats when fresh garden zucchini is available.

Ingredients:

3	c. all-purpose flour
1	tsp. salt
1	tsp. baking powder
1	tsp. baking soda
2	tsp. cinnamon
¼	tsp. ground cloves
2	c. granulated sugar
3	lg. eggs
1	c. canola oil
2	c. zucchini, grated
¼	tsp. nutmeg
1	tsp. vanilla extract
½	c. pecans, chopped

Directions:

1. Preheat oven to 325 degrees F.
2. In large bowl, sift together flour, salt, baking powder, baking soda, cinnamon, cloves; set aside.
3. In large bowl, beat eggs until foamy.
4. Add sugar, oil, zucchini, nutmeg, and vanilla.
5. Mix well with beater.
6. Add flour mixture to zucchini mixture. Add nuts.
7. Add cake mixture to each jar – about 1 cup.
8. Bake the pint jars for 35 minutes, moving the jars around in the oven so they bake evenly.
9. Start checking the cakes at 25 minutes. For 1½ pint jars, bake 1 hour and 15 minutes, start checking them at 1 hour.
10. Have your hot lids ready.

11. Take one jar at a time from the oven and place a lid on, then the ring. Tightly screw on lids.
12. Allow jars to cool on your countertop.
13. Once jars are cool, decorate with round pieces of cloth. Unscrew the ring (the lid should be sealed by now) and place a few cotton balls or a wad of batting on top of the lid (makes it poofy on top) then a piece of cloth (about 3 inches larger than the lid) on top and screw the ring back on.
14. Decorate as desired.

Holiday Gifts-in-a-Jar Cookbook
A Collection of Holiday Gifts-in-a-Jar Recipes
Gifts-in-a-Jar Cookbook Series – Book 3

Cookies

Table of Contents

Page

Brownies Mix-in-a-Jar

All chocolate lovers will enjoy this treat. And they are great to have on hand during the holiday season.

Ingredients:

- 2¼ c. white sugar
- ⅔ c. unsweetened baking cocoa
- 1¼ c. all-purpose flour
- 1 tsp. baking powder
- ½ tsp. salt
- ¾ c. pecans, chopped

Directions:

1. Pour sugar into a clean and dry 1-quart jar; press down firmly.
2. Add cocoa powder and press down firmly.
3. Combine flour, baking powder, and salt; pour into jar and press down firmly.
4. Pour in chopped pecans, making sure pecans are evenly layered in jar.

Directions for Tag

Additional Ingredients:

- ¾ c. butter, softened
- 4 eggs, slightly beaten

Directions:

1. Preheat oven to 350 degrees F.
2. Lightly grease or spray a 9 x 13-inch pan.
3. Place brownie mix into large bowl, using your hands to blend thoroughly.
4. Add butter and eggs, mixing until completely blended.
5. Spread batter into prepared pan.
6. Bake 30 minutes or until done.
7. Cool in pan.
8. Cut into 2-inch squares.

Yields: 2 dozen brownies.

Candy Bar Cookies Mix-in-a-Jar

This recipe lets you add your favorite candy bar to personalize your cookies to your own taste preference.

Ingredients:

½	c. white sugar
½	c. brown sugar
1	tsp. baking soda
2	c. all-purpose flour
1	c. your favorite candy bar, chopped

Directions:

1. Place white sugar into a wide-mouth 1-quart canning jar, packing each layer in place before adding next ingredient.
2. Add brown sugar to jar, pack down.
3. Blend baking soda and flour together, add blend to jar.
4. Place chopped candy bar on top as last of layered ingredients.
5. Close jar and seal tightly.
6. Attach a tag with mixing and baking directions.

Directions for Tag

Additional Ingredients:

¾	c. butter, softened
2	eggs, slightly beaten
1	tsp. vanilla extract

Directions:

1. Preheat oven to 350 degrees F.
2. In large bowl, cream together butter, eggs, and vanilla.
3. Add cookie mix and stir together until mixture is well blended.
4. Drop by rounded tablespoonfuls onto a baking sheet.
5. Bake 8 to 10 minutes, or until done.

Yields: 3 dozen cookies.

Candy-Coated Chocolate Cookies
Mix-in-a-Jar

These are delicious and visually appealing as well.

Ingredients:

½ tsp. baking soda
½ tsp. baking powder
2 c. all-purpose flour
1¼ c. sugar
1 c. candy-coated chocolate pieces

Directions:

1. In large bowl, blend together baking soda, baking powder, and flour.
2. Place flour mixture into a wide-mouth, 1-quart canning jar first, layer rest of ingredients into jar in order given, packing each layer in place before adding next ingredient.
3. Attach directions for mixing and baking on tag.

Directions for Tag

Additional Ingredients:

¾ c. butter, softened
2 eggs, slightly beaten
1 tsp. vanilla extract

Directions:

1. Preheat oven to 375 degrees F.
2. In large bowl, cream butter, eggs, and vanilla.
3. Add cookie mix and stir until mixture is well blended.
4. Drop by rounded tablespoonfuls onto greased baking sheet.
5. Bake 10 to 12 minutes.
6. Transfer to wire racks to cool.

Yields: 3 to 4 dozen cookies.

Chocolate Bar Oatmeal Cookies
Mix-in-a-Jar

The combination of ground oatmeal and grated chocolate makes a deliciously flavored treat.

Ingredients:

1	c. all-purpose flour
½	tsp. baking powder
½	tsp. baking soda
1½	c. whole rolled oats
1	lg. chocolate bar
½	c. white sugar
½	c. brown sugar
½	c. nuts, chopped
½	c. semisweet chocolate chips

Directions:

1. In medium bowl, mix together flour, baking powder, and baking soda.
2. Using a funnel with a wide opening pour mixture into jar, pack it down level with a heavy object.
3. Process oatmeal in blender until finely ground.
4. Grate chocolate bar and mix into ground oatmeal.
5. Pack oatmeal mixture on top of flour in jar.
6. Add white sugar, pack down, add brown sugar and pack down.
7. Layer chopped nuts on top of brown sugar.
8. Finish layering jar with chocolate chips until even with the top, and seal with a lid.
9. Attach a tag with mixing and baking directions.

Directions for Tag

Additional Ingredients:

½   c. butter, softened
1   egg, lightly beaten
½   tsp. vanilla extract

Directions:

1. Preheat oven to 375 degrees F.
2. Spoon chocolate chips and nuts into small bowl, set aside.
3. Spoon brown and white sugar into mixing bowl; add butter, cream well.
4. Add lightly beaten egg and vanilla, mix well.
5. Pour oatmeal and flour mixture into bowl, mix thoroughly.
6. Roll into walnut-size balls, place on slightly greased baking sheet 2 inches apart.
7. Bake 8 to 10 minutes, or until done.

Yields: 3 dozen cookies.

Chocolate Chip Cookies Mix-in-a-Jar

This simple classic recipe is always a favorite.

Ingredients:

1	tsp. baking powder
1	tsp. baking soda
¾	c. all-purpose flour
¼	c. sugar
¼	c. brown sugar
1¼	c. chocolate chips
½	c. brown sugar
¼	c. sugar
1	c. all-purpose flour

Directions:

1. In small bowl, blend baking powder, baking soda, and flour.
2. Place baking powder, soda, and flour mixture into a wide-mouth, 1-quart canning jar, layer rest of the ingredients in the jar in order given, packing each layer in place before adding the next ingredient.
3. Close jar with a tight-fitting lid.
4. Attach a gift card with mixing and baking directions.

Directions for Tag

Additional Ingredients:

¾	c. butter, softened
2	eggs, slightly beaten
½	tsp. vanilla extract

Directions:

1. Preheat oven to 350 degrees F.
2. In large bowl, cream butter, eggs, and vanilla.
3. Add cookie mix and stir until mixture is well blended.
4. Drop by rounded tablespoonfuls onto greased baking sheet.
5. Bake 8 to 10 minutes.
6. Transfer to wire racks to cool.

Yields: 3 to 4 dozen cookies.

Chocolate Covered Raisin Cookies
Mix-in-a-Jar

Chocolate covered raisins make a wonderful flavor addition to these cookies.

Ingredients:

1	tsp. baking powder
2	c. all-purpose flour
¼	c. brown sugar
1¼	c. chocolate covered raisins
¾	c. sugar
¼	c. semisweet chocolate chips

Directions:

1. In small bowl, blend together baking powder and flour.
2. Place flour mixture into a wide-mouth, 1-quart canning jar, layer the rest of the ingredients into jar in the order given, packing each layer in place before adding next ingredient.
3. Attach a gift card with mixing and baking directions.

Directions for Tag

Additional Ingredients:

½	c. butter, softened
2	eggs, slightly beaten
1¼	tsp. vanilla extract

Directions:

1. Preheat oven to 375 degrees F.
2. In large bowl, cream butter, eggs, and vanilla.
3. Add cookie mix and stir until mixture is blended.
4. Drop by rounded tablespoonfuls onto greased baking sheet.
5. Bake 10 to 13 minutes.
6. Transfer to wire racks to cool.

Yields: 3 dozen cookies.

Chocolate Pecan Cookies Mix-in-a-Jar

Chocolate and pecans make a great combination in this cookie mix-in-a-jar.

Ingredients:

¾   c. all-purpose flour
3   Tbs. brown sugar
½   c. sugar
1   c. pecans, chopped
3   Tbs. brown sugar
½   c. sugar
½   c. unsweetened baking cocoa
¾   c. all-purpose flour
1   tsp. baking soda

Directions:

1. Layer ingredients in order given into a wide-mouth 1-quart canning jar.
2. Pack each layer in place before adding next ingredient.
3. Attach a gift card with mixing and baking directions.

Directions for Tag

Additional Ingredients:

½   c. butter, softened
2   eggs, slightly beaten
1   tsp. vanilla extract

Directions:

1. Preheat oven to 375 degrees F.
2. In large bowl, cream butter, eggs, and vanilla.
3. Add cookie mix and stir until mixture is well blended.
4. Drop by rounded tablespoonfuls onto greased baking sheet.
5. Bake 10 to 12 minutes.
6. Transfer to wire racks to cool.

Yields: 3 dozen cookies.

Chunky Butterscotch Cookies
Mix-in-a-Jar

Butterscotch and pecans together yield deliciously aromatic and flavorful cookies.

Ingredients:

- 1   tsp. baking powder
- 1   tsp. baking soda
- 1¾   c. all-purpose flour
- ¾   c. brown sugar
- 1   tsp. ground cinnamon
- ½   c. sugar
- 1   c. butterscotch baking chips
- ½   c. pecans, chopped

Directions:

1. In small bowl, blend together baking powder, baking soda, and flour.
2. Place flour mixture into a wide-mouth, 1-quart canning jar, layer rest of ingredients into jar in order given, packing each layer in place before adding next ingredient.
3. Attach a gift card with mixing and baking directions.

Directions for Tag

Additional Ingredients:

- ¾   c. butter, softened
- 3   eggs, slightly beaten
- 1   tsp. vanilla extract

Directions:

1. Preheat oven to 375 degrees F.
2. In large bowl, cream butter, eggs, and vanilla.
3. Add cookie mix and stir until mixture is well blended.
4. Drop by rounded tablespoonfuls onto greased baking sheet.
5. Bake 11 to 13 minutes.
6. Transfer to wire racks to cool.

Chunky Chocolate Cookies
Mix-in-a-Jar

If you like a big, chunky cookie chock full of nuts and chunks of chocolate, this is the recipe for you!

Ingredients:

1	tsp. baking powder
1	tsp. baking soda
1¾	c. all-purpose flour
¾	c. brown sugar
½	c. sugar
¼	c. baking cocoa powder
½	c. pecans, chopped
1	c. chocolate chips or chunks

Directions:

1. In small bowl, blend together baking powder, baking soda, and flour.
2. Place flour mixture into a wide-mouth, 1-quart canning jar, layer rest of ingredients into jar in order given, packing each layer in place before adding next ingredient.
3. Attach a gift card with mixing and baking directions.

Directions for Tag

Additional Ingredients:

¾	c. butter, softened
3	eggs, slightly beaten
1	tsp. vanilla extract

Directions:

1. Preheat oven to 350 degrees F.
2. In large bowl, cream butter, eggs, and vanilla.
3. Add cookie mix and stir until mixture is well blended.
4. Drop by rounded tablespoonfuls onto greased baking sheet.
5. Bake 11 to 13 minutes.
6. Transfer to wire racks to cool.

Yields: 3 dozen cookies.

Hazelnut Cookies Mix-in-a-Jar

This is a crispy crunchy cookie, great for gift giving or receiving.

Ingredients:

- ½ tsp. baking powder
- ½ tsp. baking soda
- ¾ c. all-purpose flour
- ¾ c. old-fashioned oats
- ¼ c. brown sugar
- ¾ c. hazelnuts, chopped
- ¼ c. brown sugar
- 1 c. rice cereal, crisped
- ½ c. sugar

Directions:

1. In small bowl, blend together baking powder, baking soda, and flour.
2. Place flour mixture into a wide-mouth, 1-quart canning jar, layer rest of ingredients into jar in order given, packing each layer in place before adding next ingredient.
3. Attach directions for mixing and baking on the tag.

Directions for Tag

Additional Ingredients:

- ½ c. butter, softened
- 2 eggs, slightly beaten
- 1¼ tsp. vanilla extract

Directions:

1. Preheat oven to 350 degrees F.
2. In large bowl, cream butter, eggs, and vanilla.
3. Add cookie mix and stir until mixture is well blended.
4. Drop by rounded tablespoonfuls onto greased baking sheet.
5. Bake 10 to 12 minutes.
6. Transfer to wire racks to cool.

Yields: 3 to 4 dozen cookies.

Molasses Cookies Mix-in-a-Jar

I am a fan of molasses cookies, and these cookies make a nice gift.

Ingredients:

1⅓	c. sugar
1	tsp. baking soda
1	tsp. baking powder
1¼	tsp. cinnamon
½	tsp. nutmeg
¼	tsp. cloves
⅛	tsp. allspice
1	tsp. ginger
3	c. all-purpose flour

Directions:

1. Layer ingredients in the order given into a wide-mouth 1-quart canning jar.
2. Pack each layer in place before adding next ingredient.
3. Attach a gift card with mixing and baking directions.

Directions for Tag

Additional Ingredients:

¾	c. butter, softened
2	eggs, slightly beaten
¼	c. sweet molasses

Directions:

1. Preheat oven to 375 degrees F.
2. In large bowl, cream butter, eggs, and molasses.
3. Add cookie mix and stir until mixture is well blended.
4. Drop by rounded tablespoonfuls onto greased baking sheet.
5. Bake 10 to 12 minutes.
6. Transfer to wire racks to cool.

Yields: 3 dozen cookies.

Oatmeal Butterscotch Cookies
Mix-in-a-Jar

This is the traditional butterscotch oatmeal cookie that I grew up with. I hope you enjoy them as well.

Ingredients:

1	tsp. baking soda
1	c. all-purpose flour
1¼	tsp. ground cinnamon
¾	c. brown sugar
½	c. sugar
½	c. butterscotch baking chips
2	c. old-fashioned oats

Directions:

1. In small bowl, blend together baking soda, flour, and cinnamon.
2. Place flour mixture into a wide-mouth, 1-quart canning jar, layer rest of ingredients into jar in order given, packing each layer in place before adding next ingredient.
3. Attach directions for mixing and baking on the tag.

Directions for Tag

Additional Ingredients:

¾	c. butter, softened
2	eggs, slightly beaten
1¼	tsp. vanilla extract

Directions:

1. Preheat oven to 350 degrees F.
2. In large bowl, cream butter, eggs, and vanilla.
3. Add cookie mix and stir until mixture is well blended.
4. Drop by rounded tablespoonfuls onto greased baking sheet.
5. Bake 10 to 12 minutes.
6. Transfer to wire racks to cool.

Yields: 3 dozen cookies.

Oatmeal Chocolate Cookies
Mix-in-a-Jar

This is one of my favorite recipes, especially for a late-night treat.

Ingredients:

1	tsp. baking soda
1	c. all-purpose flour
¾	c. brown sugar
½	c. sugar
½	c. chocolate baking chips
2	c. old-fashioned oats
1¼	Tbs. cinnamon, ground

Directions:

1. In small bowl, blend together baking soda and flour.
2. Place flour mixture into a wide-mouth, 1-quart canning jar, layer rest of ingredients into jar in order given, packing each layer in place before adding next ingredient.
3. Attach directions for mixing and baking on the tag.

Directions for Tag

Additional Ingredients:

¾	c. butter, softened
2	eggs, slightly beaten
1¼	tsp. vanilla extract

Directions:

1. Preheat oven to 350 degrees F.
2. In large bowl, cream butter, eggs, and vanilla.
3. Add cookie mix and stir until mixture is well blended.
4. Drop by rounded tablespoonfuls onto greased baking sheet.
5. Bake 10 to 12 minutes.
6. Transfer to wire racks to cool.

Yields: 3 to 4 dozen cookies.

Oatmeal, Cranberry, and Spice Cookies Mix-in-a-Jar

This recipe makes fruity, spicy cookies that are very aromatic and hard to resist.

Ingredients:

1	tsp. baking soda
2	c. all-purpose flour
½	c. dried cranberries, chopped
½	c. sugar
1	tsp. ground cinnamon
½	tsp. ground nutmeg
½	c. brown sugar
1¼	c. old-fashioned oats

Directions:

1. In small bowl, blend together baking soda and flour.
2. Place flour mixture into a wide-mouth, 1-quart canning jar, layer rest of ingredients into jar in order given, packing each layer in place before adding next ingredient.
3. Attach directions for mixing and baking on the tag.

Directions for Tag

Additional Ingredients:

¾	c. butter softened
2	eggs, slightly beaten
1	tsp. vanilla extract

Directions:

1. Preheat oven to 350 degrees F.
2. In large bowl, cream butter, eggs, and vanilla.
3. Add cookie mix and stir until mixture is well blended.
4. Drop by rounded tablespoonfuls onto greased baking sheet.
5. Bake 10 to 12 minutes.
6. Transfer to wire racks to cool.

Yields: 3 to 4 dozen cookies.

Orange Slice Cookies Mix-in-a-Jar

These make an attractive variation for a gift-in-a-jar. Decorate your jar with a big orange and white ribbon to make it even more attractive.

Ingredients:

- ½   tsp. baking soda
- 1   tsp. baking powder
- 1¾   c. all-purpose flour
- ¾   c. sugar
- ½   c. brown sugar
- 1½   c. sugar coated orange slice candies, quartered, and wrapped in plastic wrap or sealed in a baggie

Directions:

1. In small bowl, blend together baking soda, baking powder, and flour.
2. Place flour mixture into a wide-mouth, 1-quart canning jar, layer rest of ingredients into jar in order given, packing each layer in place before adding next ingredient, and ending with wrapped candies on top.
3. Attach directions for mixing and baking to the tag.

Directions for Tag

Additional Ingredients:

- ½   c. butter, softened
- 2   eggs, slightly beaten
- 1   tsp. vanilla extract

Directions:

1. Preheat oven to 375 degrees F.
2. In large bowl, cream butter, eggs, and vanilla.
3. Remove orange slice candies from the jar and set aside.
4. Add cookie mix and stir until mixture is well blended.
5. Stir in orange slice candies.
6. Drop by rounded tablespoonfuls onto greased baking sheet.
7. Bake 12 to 14 minutes.
8. Transfer to wire racks to cool.

Yields: 3 to 4 dozen cookies.

Peanut Butter Cookies Mix-in-a-Jar

The combination of peanuts and peanut butter chips are a pleasing texture in this old classic.

Ingredients:

- 1   tsp. baking soda
- 1½   c. all-purpose flour
- ¾   c. salted peanuts, chopped
- ¾   c. brown sugar
- ¾   c. sugar
- 1   c. peanut butter chips

Directions:

1. In small bowl, blend together baking soda and flour.
2. Place flour mixture into a wide-mouth, 1-quart canning jar, layer rest of ingredients into jar in order given, packing each layer in place before adding next ingredient.
3. Attach directions for mixing and baking to the tag.

Directions for Tag

Additional Ingredients:

- ½   c. butter, softened
- 1   egg, slightly beaten
- 1   tsp. vanilla extract
- ½   c. creamy peanut butter

Directions:

1. Preheat oven to 350 degrees F.
2. In large bowl, cream butter, egg, and vanilla.
3. Blend in peanut butter.
4. Add cookie mix and stir until the mixture is well blended.
5. Drop by rounded tablespoonfuls onto a greased baking sheet.
6. Bake 11 to 13 minutes.
7. Transfer to wire racks to cool.

Yields: 3 to 4 dozen cookies.

Peanut Butter Chocolate Chip Cookies
Mix-in-a-Jar

These are easy-to-make cookies and the chocolate chips always make them popular.

Ingredients:

½	tsp. baking soda
2	c. all-purpose flour
¾	c. brown sugar
¾	c. sugar
1	c. chocolate chips

Directions:

1. In small bowl, blend together baking soda and flour.
2. Place flour mixture into a wide-mouth, 1-quart canning jar, layer rest of ingredients into jar in order given, packing each layer in place before adding next ingredient.
3. Attach directions for mixing and baking to the tag.

Directions for Tag

Additional Ingredients:

1	c. butter, softened
2	eggs, slightly beaten
1¼	tsp. vanilla extract
1	c. creamy peanut butter

Directions:

1. Preheat oven to 350 degrees F.
2. In large bowl, cream butter, eggs, and vanilla.
3. Blend in peanut butter.
4. Add cookie mix and stir until mixture is well blended.
5. Drop by rounded tablespoonfuls onto greased baking sheet.
6. Bake 9 to 11 minutes.
7. Transfer to wire racks to cool.

Yields: 3 to 4 dozen cookies.

Pecan White Chocolate Chip Cookies
Mix-in-a-Jar

Oatmeal, pecans, and white chocolate chips make an attractive gift-in-a-jar that is also very tasty.

Ingredients:

½	tsp. baking soda
½	tsp. baking powder
¾	c. all-purpose flour
¾	c. old-fashioned oats
¾	c. pecans, chopped
1	c. white chocolate chips
½	c. brown sugar
½	c. sugar

Directions:

1. In small bowl, blend together baking soda, baking powder, and flour.
2. Place flour mixture into a wide-mouth, 1-quart canning jar, layer rest of ingredients into jar in order given, packing each layer in place before adding next ingredient.
3. Attach a gift card with mixing and baking directions.

Directions for Tag

Additional Ingredients:

½	c. butter, softened
2	eggs, slightly beaten
1¼	tsp. vanilla extract

Directions:

1. Preheat oven to 350 degrees F.
2. In large bowl, cream butter, eggs, and vanilla.
3. Add cookie mix and stir until mixture is well blended.
4. Drop by rounded tablespoonfuls onto greased baking sheet.
5. Bake 10 to 12 minutes.
6. Transfer to wire racks to cool.

Yields: 3 to 4 dozen cookies.

Raisin Crunch Cookies Mix-in-a-Jar

These make great-tasting oatmeal raisin cookies with the added texture of corn cereal.

Ingredients:

1	tsp. baking soda
1	tsp. baking powder
1¼	c. all-purpose flour
¾	c. brown sugar
½	c. sugar
½	c. raisins
1¼	c. coconut, flaked
1	c. flaky corn cereal, crushed
¾	c. old-fashioned oats

Directions:

1. In small bowl, blend together baking soda, baking powder, and flour.
2. Place flour mixture into a wide-mouth, 1-quart canning jar, layer rest of ingredients into jar in order given, packing each layer in place before adding next ingredient.
3. Attach a gift card with mixing and baking directions.

Directions for Tag

Additional Ingredients:

¾	c. butter, softened
2	eggs, slightly beaten
1¼	tsp. vanilla extract

Directions:

1. Preheat oven to 350 degrees F.
2. In large bowl, cream together butter, eggs, and vanilla.
3. Add cookie mix and stir until mixture is well blended.
4. Drop by rounded tablespoonfuls onto greased baking sheet.
5. Bake 10 to 12 minutes.
6. Transfer to wire racks to cool.

Yields: 3 to 4 dozen cookies.

Snicker Doodle Cookies
Mix-in-a-Jar

Snicker Doodles are one of my nephew's favorite cookies and this is an easy to make version.

Ingredients:

1	tsp. baking soda
2	tsp. cream of tartar
2¾	c. all-purpose flour
¼	c. brown sugar
1¼	c. sugar

Directions:

1. In small bowl, blend together baking soda, cream of tartar, and flour.
2. Place flour mixture into a wide-mouth, 1-quart canning jar, layer rest of ingredients into jar in order given, packing each layer in place before adding next ingredient.
3. Attach a gift card with mixing and baking directions.

Directions for Tag

Additional Ingredients:

1	c. butter, softened
2	eggs, slightly beaten
½	c. sugar
1¼	Tbs. cinnamon

Directions:

1. Preheat oven to 375 degrees F.
2. In large bowl, cream butter until light, add eggs and beat until mixture is smooth.
3. Add cookie mix and continue to beat until dough begins to form.
4. Combine sugar and cinnamon in a small bowl.
5. Shape dough into 1-inch balls and roll in cinnamon sugar blend.
6. Arrange on ungreased baking sheet and bake 10 to 15 minutes or until light tan.
7. Transfer to wire racks to cool.

Yields: 4 to 5 dozen cookies.

Toffee Candy Bar Cookies Mix-in-a-Jar

Toffee candy bars have been very popular for years and this recipe for a mix-in-a-jar makes a great gift and great cookies.

Ingredients:

1	tsp. baking soda
2	c. all-purpose flour
½	c. sugar
½	c. brown sugar
1	c. toffee candy bars, coarsely chopped

Directions:

1. In small bowl, blend together baking soda and flour.
2. Place flour mixture into a wide-mouth, 1-quart canning jar, layer rest of ingredients into jar in order given, packing each layer in place before adding next ingredient.
3. Attach directions for mixing and baking on the tag.

Directions for Tag

Additional Ingredients:

¾	c. butter, softened
2	eggs, slightly beaten
1	tsp. vanilla extract

Directions:

1. Preheat oven to 350 degrees F.
2. In large bowl, cream butter, eggs, and vanilla.
3. Add cookie mix and stir until mixture is well blended.
4. Drop by rounded tablespoonfuls onto greased baking sheet.
5. Bake 10 to 12 minutes.
6. Transfer to wire racks to cool.

Yields: 3 to 4 dozen cookies.

Trail Mix Cookies Mix-in-a-Jar

These make a nutritious cookie. Make sure you use fresh wheat germ and keep refrigerated until you are ready to use.

Ingredients:

1	tsp. baking powder
¾	c. all-purpose flour
½	c. brown sugar
½	c. sugar
¾	c. wheat germ
½	c. rolled oats
1	c. raisins
⅓	c. coconut, flaked
¾	c. pecans, chopped

Directions:

1. In small bowl, blend together baking powder and flour.
2. Place flour mixture into a wide-mouth, 1-quart canning jar, layer rest of ingredients into jar in order given, packing each layer in place before adding next ingredient.
3. Attach a gift card with mixing and baking directions.

Directions for Tag

Ingredients:

½	c. butter, softened
2	eggs, slightly beaten
1¼	tsp. vanilla extract

Directions:

1. Preheat oven to 350 degrees F.
2. In large bowl, cream butter, eggs, and vanilla.
3. Add cookie mix and stir until mixture is well blended.
4. Drop by rounded tablespoonfuls onto greased baking sheet.
5. Bake 12 to 14 minutes.
6. Transfer to wire racks to cool.

Yields: 3 to 4 dozen cookies.

Triple Chocolate Chip Cookies
Mix-in-a-Jar

Two kinds of chocolate chips blend with cocoa for a triple chocolate cookie.

Ingredients:

- ½ tsp. baking soda
- 1¼ c. all-purpose flour
- 2 Tbs. plus 2 tsp. cocoa powder
- 6 Tbs. sugar
- ⅓ c. brown sugar
- ½ c. white chocolate chips
- ¾ c. pecans, chopped
- ½ c. chocolate chips

Directions:

1. In small bowl, blend together baking soda and flour.
2. Place flour mixture into a wide-mouth, 1-quart canning jar, layer rest of ingredients into jar in order given, packing each layer in place before adding next ingredient.
3. Attach a gift card with mixing and baking directions.

Directions for Tag

Additional Ingredients:

- ½ c. butter, softened
- 2 eggs, slightly beaten
- 1 Tbs. cream
- 1¼ tsp. vanilla extract

Directions:

1. Preheat oven to 350 degrees F.
2. In large bowl, cream butter, eggs, cream, and vanilla.
3. Add cookie mix and stir until mixture is well blended.
4. Drop by rounded tablespoonfuls onto greased baking sheet.
5. Bake 8 to 10 minutes.
6. Transfer to wire racks to cool.

Yields: 3 to 4 dozen cookies.

Vanilla and Chocolate Chip Cookies Mix-in-a-Jar

The blend of chocolate chips makes a tasty chocolate treat.

Ingredients:

1	tsp. baking soda
1	tsp. baking powder
2	c. all-purpose flour
⅓	c. brown sugar
⅔	c. sugar
1	c. semisweet chocolate chips
½	c. white chocolate chips

Directions:

1. In medium bowl, blend together baking soda, baking powder, and flour.
2. Place flour mixture into a wide-mouth, 1-quart canning jar, layer rest of ingredients into jar in order given, packing each layer in place before adding next ingredient.
3. Attach a gift card with mixing and baking directions.

Directions for Tag

Additional Ingredients:

¾	c. butter, softened
2	eggs, slightly beaten
1¼	tsp. vanilla extract

Directions:

1. Preheat oven to 350 degrees F.
2. In large bowl, cream together butter, eggs, and vanilla.
3. Add cookie mix and stir until mixture is well blended.
4. Drop by rounded tablespoonfuls onto greased baking sheet.
5. Bake 15 to 18 minutes.
6. Transfer to wire racks to cool.

Yields: 3 to 4 dozen cookies.

White Chocolate Macadamia Nut Cookies Mix-in-a-Jar

This is a tasty, melt-in-your-mouth cookie, using delicious macadamia nuts and white chocolate chunks.

Ingredients:

½	tsp. baking soda
½	tsp. baking powder
2	c. all-purpose flour
1¼	c. sugar
¾	c. macadamia nuts, chopped
1	c. white chocolate chunks

Directions:

1. In medium bowl, blend together baking soda, baking powder, and flour.
2. Place flour mixture into a wide-mouth, 1-quart canning jar, layer rest of ingredients into jar in order given, packing each layer in place before adding next ingredient.
3. Attach a gift tag with mixing and baking directions.

Directions for Tag

Additional Ingredients:

1	c. butter, softened
2	eggs, slightly beaten
2	tsp. vanilla extract

Directions:

1. Preheat oven to 375 degrees F.
2. In large bowl, cream together butter, eggs, and vanilla.
3. Add cookie mix and stir until mixture is well blended.
4. Drop by rounded tablespoonfuls onto greased baking sheet.
5. Bake 12 to 14 minutes.
6. Transfer to wire racks to cool.

Yields: 3 to 4 dozen cookies.

Yuletide Sand Art Cookies Mix-in-a-Jar

Children of all ages love sand art and this theme makes a colorful cookie mix-in-a-jar.

Ingredients:

1	c. vanilla chips
1	c. dried cranberries
½	c. red sugar
½	c. green sugar
2	c. flour
½	tsp. baking powder
½	tsp. baking soda
¼	tsp. salt

Directions:

1. Layer ingredients in jar in order given packing each layer in place before adding next ingredient.

Directions for Tag

Additional Ingredients:

1	c. butter
2	eggs
2	tsp. vanilla extract
½	tsp. almond extract

Directions:

1. Preheat oven to 350 degrees F.
2. In small bowl, cream butter and sugars. Add eggs, extract, and dry ingredients stir to combine.
3. Drop by teaspoonfuls onto baking sheet.
4. Bake 10 to 12 minutes or until golden brown.

Holiday Gifts-in-a-Jar Cookbook
A Collection of Holiday Gifts-in-a-Jar Recipes
Gifts-in-a-Jar Cookbook Series – Book 3

Scones

Table of Contents

Page

Blueberry Scone Mix-in-a-Jar

Blueberries are a welcome treat in this delicious scone mix. This makes a great gift for any occasion.

Ingredients:

- 2   c. all-purpose flour
- ⅓   c. sugar
- 1   c. dried blueberries
- ¼   c. nonfat dry milk
- 2   tsp. baking powder
- 1   tsp. dried lemon peel
- ¼   tsp. salt

Directions:

1. Starting with first ingredient, layer ingredients into clean, dry wide-mouth quart jar in order given; press each layer firmly with flat-bottomed object, making layers as level as possible.
2. Secure lid, label, and store in cool dry place for up to 12 months.
3. For gift-giving, decorate lid as desired.
4. Copy instructions and attach to jar.

Yields: 1 quart jar.

Directions for Tag

Additional Ingredients:

- 1   jar Blueberry Scone Mix
- ⅓   c. butter, softened
- 1   egg, beaten
- ¼   c. cold water

Directions:

1. Preheat oven to 400 degrees F.
2. In large bowl, place contents of jar and stir.
3. Cut in butter until mixture resembles coarse crumbs.
4. Stir in egg and enough water to just moisten; form into ball.
5. On lightly floured surface, gently knead dough 12 to 15 times, pat into ½-inch-thick circle.
6. Using 2½-inch biscuit or cookie cutter, cut rounds from dough.
7. Place rounds 1 inch apart on ungreased baking sheet.
8. Bake 12 to 15 minutes or until lightly browned.
9. Serve warm.

Yields: 10 to 12 scones.

Chocolate Chip Scone Mix-in-a-Jar

Easy homemade scones complete with chocolate chips can be made.

Ingredients:

2	c. all-purpose flour
2	tsp. baking powder
¼	tsp. ground cinnamon
¼	tsp. baking soda
¼	tsp. salt
½	c. sugar
1	c. miniature semisweet chocolate chips
¾	c. golden raisins

Directions:

1. In medium bowl, combine flour, baking powder, cinnamon, soda, and salt; stir well.
2. Pour into clean, dry 1-quart wide-mouth jar; pack down well.
3. Add sugar, chips, and raisins in order given; press each layer firmly with flat-bottomed object, making layers as level as possible.
4. Secure lid, label, and store in cool, dry place.
5. For gift-giving, decorate lid as desired.
6. Copy instructions and attach to jar.

Yields: 1 quart jar.

Directions for Tag

Additional Ingredients:

1	jar Chocolate Chip Scone Mix
½	c. butter, cut into small pieces
½	c. buttermilk
2	eggs
½	tsp. vanilla extract
1	Tbs. milk

Directions:

1. Preheat oven to 350 degrees F.
2. Line two baking sheets with parchment paper, or grease well; set aside.
3. In large bowl, pour contents of jar and stir.
4. Cut butter into flour mixture with pastry cutter or two knives until mixture is crumbly.
5. Combine buttermilk, 1 egg, and vanilla in small bowl; mix well.
6. Add to dry ingredients, mixing gently until dough comes together.
7. Spoon dough onto baking sheets, using 2 tablespoons dough for each scone, leaving 1 inch between scones.
8. Combine remaining egg and milk in small bowl; brush over tops of scones.
9. Bake 12 to 14 minutes or until scones are golden brown.
10. Transfer to wire rack to cool 5 minutes.
11. Serve warm or at room temperature.

Yields: 24 scones.

Cinnamon-Raisin Scone Mix-in-a-Jar

The fragrance of cinnamon cooking in the oven will be a welcome treat when baking this batch of scone mix-in-a-jar.

Ingredients:

- 2   c. all-purpose flour
- ⅓   c. sugar
- 1   c. dark raisins
- ¼   c. nonfat dry milk
- 2   tsp. baking powder
- 1   tsp. ground cinnamon
- ¼   tsp. salt

Directions:

1. Starting with first ingredient, layer ingredients into clean, dry wide-mouth quart jar in order given; press each layer firmly with flat-bottomed object, making layers as level as possible.
2. Secure lid, label, and store in cool dry place for up to 12 months.
3. For gift-giving, decorate lid as desired.
4. Copy instructions and attach to jar.

Yields: 1 quart jar.

Directions for Tag

Additional Ingredients:

- 1   jar Cinnamon-Raisin Scone Mix
- ⅓   c. butter, softened
- 1   egg, beaten
- ¼   c. cold water

Directions:

1. Preheat oven to 400 degrees F.
2. In large bowl, place contents of jar and stir.
3. Cut in butter until mixture resembles coarse crumbs.
4. Stir in egg and enough water to just moisten; form into ball.
5. On lightly floured surface, gently knead dough 12 to 15 times, pat into ½-inch-thick circle.
6. Using 2½-inch biscuit or cookie cutter, cut rounds from dough.
7. Place rounds 1 inch apart on ungreased baking sheet.
8. Bake 12 to 15 minutes or until lightly browned.
9. Serve warm.

Yields: 10 to 12 scones.

Cornmeal, Sunflower, and Cranberry Scone Mix-in-a-Jar

Cranberries and roasted sunflower kernels add nice flavor to this delicious scone mix-in-a-jar.

Ingredients:

1½	c. all-purpose flour
1	Tbs. baking powder
¼	tsp. salt
⅓	c. yellow cornmeal
3	Tbs. corn grits (polenta)
½	c. sugar
¾	c. salted roasted sunflower kernels
¾	c. sweetened dried cranberries

Directions:

1. In medium bowl, combine flour, baking powder, and salt; stir well.
2. Pour into clean, dry 1-quart wide-mouth jar; pack down well.
3. Combine cornmeal and grits; add to jar and pack down.
4. Add sugar, sunflower kernels, and cranberries in order given; press each layer firmly with flat-bottomed object, making layers as level as possible.
5. Secure lid, label, and store in cool, dry place.
6. For gift-giving, decorate lid as desired.
7. Copy instructions and attach to jar.

Yields: 1 quart jar.

Directions for Tag

Additional Ingredients:

1   jar Cornmeal, Sunflower, and Cranberry Scone Mix
½   c. butter, cut into small pieces
⅔-¾ c. half-and-half or milk

Directions:

1. Preheat oven to 425 degrees F.
2. Line baking sheet with parchment paper, or grease well; set aside.
3. In large bowl, pour contents of jar and stir.
4. Cut butter into flour mixture with pastry cutter or two knives.
5. When mixture is crumbly, add half-and-half by ¼ cupfuls, mixing gently until dough comes together. (Dough should have same consistency as baking powder biscuits).
6. If dough is too dry, add more half-and-half, 1 tablespoon at a time.
7. Scoop out dough to ¼ cupfuls and turn out onto baking sheet, leaving 1 inch between scones.
8. Bake 15 to 17 minutes or until scones are golden brown.
9. Cool on baking sheet 5 minutes, then transfer to wire rack.
10. Serve warm or at room temperature.

Yields: 14 to 18 scones.

Oat and Pecan Scone Mix-in-a-Jar

Oatmeal adds wonderful texture and flavor to this scone mix. They make a welcome treat to anyone receiving this gift.

Ingredients:

¾   c. toasted old-fashioned oats (directions below)
1   c. chopped toasted pecans (directions below)
1½   c. all-purpose flour
2½   tsp. baking powder
1   tsp. ground cinnamon
½   tsp. baking soda
¼   tsp. ground ginger
¼   tsp. salt
½   c. packed brown sugar
½   c. raisins or currants

Directions for toasting oats:

1. Spread oats in single layer in heavy-bottomed skillet.
2. Cook over medium heat 1 to 2 minutes, stirring frequently, until oats just start to turn golden.
3. Remove from skillet immediately.
4. Cool before using.

Directions for toasting pecans:

1. Spread pecans in single layer in heavy-bottomed skillet.
2. Cook over medium heat 1 to 2 minutes, stirring frequently, until pecans are lightly browned.
3. Remove from skillet immediately.
4. Cool before using.

Directions for mix:

1. In medium bowl, combine flour, baking powder, cinnamon, soda, ginger, and salt; stir well.
2. Pour into clean, dry 1-quart wide-mouth jar; pack down well.
3. Add brown sugar, toasted oats, toasted pecans, and raisins; press each layer firmly with flat-bottomed object, making layers as level as possible.
4. Secure lid, label, and store in cool, dry place.
5. For gift-giving, decorate lid as desired.
6. Copy instructions and attach to jar.

Yields: 1 quart jar.

Directions for Tag

Additional Ingredients:

1	jar Oat and Pecan Scone Mix
½	c. butter, cut into small pieces
⅔-¾	c. half-and-half or milk
2	tsp. sugar

Directions:

1. Preheat oven to 425 degrees F.
2. Line baking sheet with parchment paper, or grease well; set aside.
3. Pour contents of jar into large bowl; stir until ingredients are evenly mixed.
4. Bake 15 to 17 minutes or until scones are golden brown.

Walnut-Ginger Scone Mix-in-a-Jar

If you enjoy ginger and cinnamon you will appreciate this scone recipe. These scones also add a delicious fragrance to your kitchen.

Ingredients:

1	c. coarsely chopped toasted walnuts (directions below)
1	c. all-purpose flour
1	Tbs. baking powder
½	tsp. salt
1	c. whole-wheat flour
½	tsp. ground cinnamon
¼	c. sugar
¾	c. diced crystallized ginger (¼-in. pieces)
½	c. currants

Directions for toasting walnuts:

1. Spread walnuts in single layer in heavy-bottomed skillet.
2. Cook over medium heat 1 to 2 minutes, stirring frequently, until walnuts are lightly browned.
3. Remove from skillet immediately.
4. Cool before using.

Directions for mix:

1. In small bowl, combine flour, baking powder, and salt; stir well.
2. Pour into clean, dry 1-quart wide-mouth jar; pack down well.
3. Combine whole-wheat flour and cinnamon; add to jar and pack down.
4. Add sugar, ginger, toasted walnuts, and currants; press each layer firmly with flat-bottomed object, making layers as level as possible.

5. Secure lid, label, and store in cool, dry place.
6. For gift-giving, decorate lid as desired.
7. Copy instructions and attach to jar.

Yields: 1 quart jar.

Directions for Tag

Additional Ingredients:

1   jar Walnut-Ginger Scone mix
½   c. butter, cut into small pieces
¾-1 c. half-and-half
1   tsp. sugar

Directions:

1. Preheat oven to 425 degrees F.
2. Line baking sheet with parchment paper, or grease well; set aside.
3. In large bowl, pour contents of jar and stir.
4. Cut butter into flour mixture with pastry cutter or two knives.
5. When mixture is crumbly, add half-and-half by ¼ cupfuls, mixing gently until dough comes together.
6. Pat into 10-inch circle on prepared baking sheet.
7. Sprinkle with sugar; cut circle into 10 wedges.
8. Bake 15 minutes, then pull wedges apart, leaving 1 inch between wedges.
9. Return to oven and bake 6 to 8 minutes longer or until scones are golden brown.
10. Cool on baking sheet 10 minutes.
11. Transfer to wire rack to cool completely.

Holiday Gifts-in-a-Jar Cookbook

A Collection of Holiday Gifts-in-a-Jar Recipes
Gifts-in-a-Jar Cookbook Series – Book 3

Seasonings

Table of Contents

Page

Bread Coating Mix-in-a-Jar

This makes a flavorful coating to give as a gift-in-a-jar.

Ingredients:

3¼ c. dry bread crumbs, crushed
⅓   c. flour
6   Tbs. paprika
4   tsp. salt
2   tsp. onion powder
2   tsp. ground oregano
1   tsp. ground red pepper
¾   tsp. garlic powder
¼   c. dried parsley flakes

Directions:

1. Mix dry ingredients together in a 1-quart jar.
2. Store in tightly covered container.

Yields: 4 cups mix.

Directions for Tag

Additional Ingredients:

⅓   c. butter, melted
     milk
     your choice chicken, pork chops or fish

Directions:

1. Preheat oven to 400 degrees F.
2. Place chicken into melted butter and milk to coat, dip into coating.
3. Arrange in a single layer in ungreased shallow baking dish.
4. Bake 50 to 60 minutes or until tender and brown.
5. Note: Use same method for pork chops or fish and bake until done.

Cajun Spice Seasoning Mix-in-a-Jar

This makes a great gift for those who enjoy the flavors of Cajun foods.

Ingredients for mix:

¾	c. salt
¼	c. ground cayenne pepper
2	Tbs. ground white pepper
2	Tbs. ground black pepper
2	Tbs. paprika
2	Tbs. onion powder
2	Tbs. garlic powder

Directions:

1. While holding a pint canning jar at an angle, add ingredients to create a "sand art" look. The salt and cayenne may be divided into smaller portions and used to separate other spices. I found it simplest to use 7 cups (one with each spice in it) and add them to my jar with a spoon, as I want to create the special look.
2. Place in a small, pretty jar tied with a ribbon.

Directions for Tag

1. Use to taste for seasoning chicken, seafood, steak, or vegetables.

Creole Seasoning Mix-in-a-Jar

This makes a tasty gift for those who enjoy the flavors of Creole or Cajun foods.

Ingredients for mix:

3	Tbs. paprika
2	Tbs. garlic powder
1	Tbs. salt
1	Tbs. onion powder
1	Tbs. dried oregano
1	Tbs. dried thyme
1	Tbs. cayenne pepper
1	Tbs. pepper

Directions:

1. In small bowl, combine all ingredients.
2. Place in a small, pretty jar tied with a ribbon.

Directions for Tag

1. Use to taste for seasoning chicken, seafood, steak, or vegetables.

Favorite Fish Seasoning Mix-in-a-Jar

Our family loves fish and this makes a great tasting fish seasoning mix.

Ingredients:

2½ c. yellow cornmeal
1¼ c. all-purpose flour
3   tsp. paprika
2   tsp. dried parsley flakes, crushed
1   tsp. salt
1½ tsp. celery salt
1½ tsp. onion salt
1   tsp. lemon pepper
½   tsp. ground red pepper

Directions:

1. In large bowl, combine all ingredients and mix well.
2. Store in a glass jar.

Yields: 3¾ cups mix, should coat 4 pounds fresh fish.

Directions for Tag

Additional Ingredients:

1   egg
1   c. buttermilk
4   lb. fish (your favorite variety)
     canola oil, for frying

Directions:

1. In deep skillet, heat 1½ inches of canola oil to 375 degrees F.
2. In small bowl, combine 1 egg and 1 cup buttermilk.
3. Dip fish into egg mixture.
4. Place seasoning mix in a bag and shake dipped fish pieces one by one, until well coated.
5. Fry until fish is golden brown and flakes easily with fork.
6. Drain on paper towels and serve.

Ranch Style Dressing and Dip
Mix-in-a-Jar

This is a delicious mix that is easily made from ingredients most of us have right in our own pantries. Place in a small jar, and tie with festive ribbons for decorating according to the occasion.

Ingredients:

- 1½ Tbs. dried parsley
- 1 Tbs. salt
- ½ Tbs. dried chives
- ¼ Tbs. dried oregano
- ¼ Tbs. dried tarragon
- ½ Tbs. garlic powder
- ½ Tbs. lemon pepper

Directions:

1. Layer all ingredients in a small jar or combine all ingredients and place in a small jar with an airtight cover.

Directions for Tag

Additional Ingredients:

- ½ c. mayonnaise
- ½ c. buttermilk
- 1 Tbs. mix

To Make Dressing or Dip:

1. Whisk all ingredients together.
2. Refrigerate one hour before serving for dressing, or two hours for dip.

Holiday Gifts-in-a-Jar Cookbook
A Collection of Holiday Gifts-in-a-Jar Recipes
Gifts-in-a-Jar Cookbook Series – Book 3

Side Dishes

Table of Contents

Page

Curried Rice Mix-in-a-Jar

This recipe is one of our family's favorites with a tasty Asian flavor and is great for use as a last minute side dish.

Ingredients:

1	c. long-grain rice
1	chicken bouillon cube, crumbled
2	Tbs. dried minced onion
¼	c. raisins
½	tsp. curry powder

Directions:

1. Layer the ingredients in the order given in a 1½ cup jar.

Directions for Tag

Ingredients per serving:

1	jar Curried Rice Mix
2½	c. water

Directions:

1. In medium saucepan, bring water to boil; add rice mix.
2. Cover and reduce heat; simmer 20 minutes.

Greek Pasta-in-a-Jar

This recipe is very easy to make and so colorful to see in the jar.

Ingredients for Easy Lemon Vinaigrette:

½   c. olive oil
    juice from 1 large lemon
    good pinch of salt
    couple grinds of black pepper

Ingredients for Salad:

2   Tbs. Easy Lemon Vinaigrette (see below)
1   c. cherry tomatoes
¼   c. red onion, chopped
1   c. cucumber, chopped
½   c. goat feta, crumbled
2   oz. rigatoni, cooked
½   c. mixed greens
½   c. fresh mint, chopped

Directions for Easy Lemon Vinaigrette:

1. Combine ingredients in small bowl.

Directions for Salad:

1. The ingredients are listed in layering order. Vinaigrette on the bottom, tomatoes, red onion, and so on until you top the jar off with your fresh mint.
2. Secure the lid and store for later. Shake it up and enjoy!

Directions for Tag

1. Shake all ingredients together in a small container.

Herbed Rice Mix-in-a-Jar

This makes a unique gift-in-a-jar and is great for use as a last minute side dish.

Ingredients:

3	lbs. long grain rice
2	c. dried celery flakes
1	c. dried minced onion
¼	c. dried parsley flakes
3	Tbs. dried chives
1	Tbs. dried tarragon
3	tsp. salt
2	tsp. pepper

Directions:

1. In medium bowl, combine all ingredients; mix well.
2. Place 2 cups each in 1-pint glass jars.

Yields: 40 servings, ¼ cup dried rice mix per serving.

Directions for Tag

Ingredients per serving:

½	c. water
1	Tbs. butter

Directions:

1. To prepare one serving of rice: In saucepan over medium heat, bring water and butter to a boil.
2. Add ¼ cup rice mixture.
3. Reduce heat; cover and simmer for 20 minutes.
4. Remove from heat; let stand for 5 minutes or until liquid is absorbed.
5. Fluff with a fork.
6. To prepare more than 1 serving, multiply the rice mix, water, and butter by the total number or desired servings and cook as directed.

Hush Puppy Mix-in-a-Jar

If you haven't had hush puppies, you are missing a treat. These are often served with fish dinners. This makes a nice gift, just place it in a pretty jar or tie a plain jar with a pretty ribbon.

Ingredients:

- 1¾ c. yellow cornmeal
- ¾   c. all-purpose flour
- 3   Tbs. dried minced onion
- 1   tsp. baking powder
- 1   tsp. sugar
- 1   tsp. salt
- ½   tsp. baking soda
- ¼   tsp. ground red pepper

Directions:

1. In medium bowl, combine all ingredients and mix well.
2. Store in a glass jar.

Yields: 2¾ cups mix.

Directions for Tag

Additional Ingredients:

- 1½ c. buttermilk
- 1   egg, beaten
  canola oil

Directions:

1. In deep skillet, heat 1½ inches canola oil to 350 degrees F.
2. In medium bowl, combine mix with 1½ cups buttermilk and 1 beaten egg; stir until well blended.
3. Drop mixture by spoonfuls into hot oil.
4. Fry until golden brown and thoroughly cooked through.
5. Drain on paper towels and serve.

Scalloped Potatoes in-a-Jar

This is a quick and easy recipe when gathering with family and friends.

Ingredients:

- 3   c. dehydrated potatoes
- 2   pkg. sauce mix (6 Tbs.)
- ⅓   c. nonfat dry milk

Directions:

1. Place potatoes into the bottom of the jar. Place these ingredients into a 1-quart jar.
2. Place sauce mix and dry milk into small zip baggies, then sealed, with the air removed.
3. Add the baggie of mix on top.
4. Place lid on jar and store in a cool dry place until ready to use.

Directions for Tag

Ingredients per serving:

- 3   Tbs. butter
- 2¾ c. boiling water

Directions:

1. Preheat oven to 400 degrees F.
2. In medium size ungreased casserole dish, pour in potatoes and sprinkle sauce mix on top. Dot with butter; stir in boiling water.
3. Bake 30 to 35 minutes or until tender.

Holiday Gifts-in-a-Jar Cookbook
A Collection of Holiday Gifts-in-a-Jar Recipes
Gifts-in-a-Jar Cookbook Series – Book 3

Soups

Table of Contents

Page

Dreaming of a White Christmas Soup
Mix-in-a-Jar

This unique soup mix makes a delightful welcome gift. You can give the canned chicken wrapped to make the gift complete.

Ingredients:

1	pkg. regular country gravy mix (2.75 oz.)
2	Tbs. chicken bouillon granules
2	Tbs. dried minced onion
2	Tbs. dried celery flakes
2	tsp. dried parsley flakes

2½ - 3 c. uncooked wide egg noodles or other pasta

Directions:

1. Pour gravy mix into wide-mouth quart jar.
2. In small bowl, stir together bouillon granules, onion, celery, and parsley.
3. Pour into jar to make second layer. Add noodles.
4. Seal tightly.

Directions for Tag

Additional Ingredients:

8	c. water
1	can cooked and chopped chicken (10 oz. or two 6 oz.)

Directions:

1. Empty contents of jar into a 4-quart saucepan or Dutch oven.
2. Add 8 cups water; heat to boiling on high.
3. Reduce heat to medium; add one 10-ounce or two 6-ounce cans cooked and chopped chicken.
4. Cover and simmer for 5 to 6 minutes or until noodles are tender, stirring occasionally.

Farmhouse Soup Mix-in-a-Jar

This mix makes a wonderful comfort soup that will be enjoyed by adults and children. Enjoy.

Ingredients:

2	Tbs. dried minced onion
2	Tbs. dried parsley flakes
2	tsp. salt
½	tsp. lemon pepper
2	Tbs. beef bouillon flakes
½	c. quick-cook barley
½	c. dried split peas
½	c. cup rice, uncooked, do not use instant
½	c. cup dry lentils
½	c. cup alphabet pasta, uncooked
1	c. flavored spiral, macaroni, uncooked

Directions:

1. Layer all ingredients in a mason jar and store in cool, dry place.

Directions for Tag

Additional Ingredients:

1	jar Farmhouse Soup Mix
3	qts. water
2	stalks celery, chopped
2	carrots, sliced
1	c. cabbage, shredded
2	c. tomatoes, diced

Directions:

1. Put all ingredients into a stockpot over medium-low heat.
2. Cover and simmer about 1 hour, or until vegetables are tender.

Holiday Bean Soup Mix-in-a-Jar

This makes a healthy gift-in-a-jar that is also great without the ham hock, as a vegetarian version.

Ingredients:

1   lb. dried black beans
1   lb. dried red beans
1   lb. dried kidney beans
1   lb. dried navy beans
1   lb. dried great northern beans
1   lb. dried baby lima beans
1   lb. dried large lima beans
1   lb. dried pinto beans
1   lb. dried green split peas
1   lb. dried yellow split peas
1   lb. dried black-eyed peas
1   lb. dried green lentils
1   lb. dried brown lentils

Directions:

1. In large bowl, combine beans and mix.
2. Pour 2 cups of bean mix into pretty jars (16-oz. jars hold 2 cups bean mix).
3. Give with the following recipe for holiday bean soup.
4. You could also layer the beans in the jar for a prettier effect.
5. Just put a little of each of the beans in until you fill it to the top.

Directions for Tag

Additional Ingredients:

1	jar Holiday Bean Soup Mix
1	smoked ham hock (optional)
2	cans stewed tomatoes (14.5 oz each)
1	med. onion, chopped
1	clove garlic, minced
1	bay leaf
6	c. water
¼	c. fresh parsley
1	Tbs. red wine vinegar
2	tsp. salt
1	tsp. chili powder
1	tsp. cumin seed

Directions:

1. In large pot, cover beans with water and soak overnight.
2. Drain beans and place in a stockpot.
3. Add ham hock (optional), tomatoes, onion, garlic, bay leaf, and 6 cups water.
4. Bring to a boil over medium-high heat, cover and simmer 1 hour or until beans are tender.
5. Remove bay leaf before serving.

Yields: 11 cups soup.

Instant Potato Soup Mix-in-a-Jar

This is actually quite tasty and is a welcome gift for those on the run, and for those busy college students.

Ingredients:

1¾	c. instant mashed potatoes
1½	c. dry milk
2	Tbs. instant chicken bouillon
2	tsp. dried minced onion
1	tsp. dried parsley
¼	tsp. ground white pepper
¼	tsp. dried thyme
⅛	tsp. turmeric
1½	tsp. seasoning salt

Directions:

1. To make this gift attractive, you can layer the ingredients as you place them into a wide-mouth 1-quart canning jar (make 1 jar), or mix them all together in a large bowl then place them in a jar.
2. Seal tightly.

Directions for Tag

Additional Ingredients:

1	c. water

Directions:

1. Place ½ cup of mix in soup bowl and add 1 cup boiling water, stirring until smooth.
2. You can substitute part milk for the water, add a pat of butter if you like a richer taste.

Onion Soup Mix-in-a-Jar

This is a great soup to have on hand any time of the year.

Ingredients:

- 3   onion bouillon cubes, crushed
- 1   beef bouillon cube, crushed
- 2   tsp. cornstarch
- ⅓   c. instant onion flakes
- 2   dashes pepper

Directions:

1. Put all ingredients in a mason jar and store in a cool, dry place.

Directions for Tag

Additional Ingredients:

- 4   c. cold water
- 1   Tbs. butter

Directions:

1. Empty into a pot and gradually stir in 4 cups cold water and 1 tablespoon butter. Bring to boil, reduce heat and cover. Simmer 20 minutes.
2. Ladle soup into ovenproof bowls, sprinkle with croutons or toasted bread. Then add one slice provolone cheese. Briefly put bowls under a broiler to melt cheese. Serve.

Yields: 4 1-cup servings.

Pasta Soup Mix-in-a-Jar

This is a delicious soup mix that many will use it simply as a decoration in their kitchen.

Ingredients:

2	Tbs. Parmesan Cheese, grated
1	Tbs. onion flakes
1	Tbs. powdered chicken soup base
1	tsp. dried parsley
½	tsp. oregano
1	dash garlic powder
½	c. macaroni of your choice
¼	c. lentils, dry
¼	c. dried mushrooms, chopped

Instructions:

1. In small bowl, combine Parmesan Cheese, onion flakes, soup base, parsley, oregano, and garlic powder together.
2. In a 1-pint jar, layer ingredients in this order, spice mixture, macaroni, lentils, and mushrooms. Store with tightly sealed lid, until needed.
3. Place following recipe on a card and attach to your decorated soup mix jar to give as a gift.

Directions for Tag

Instructions:

1. In 2-quart saucepan, combine contents of jar with 3 cups water.
2. Bring to a boil, reduce heat.
3. Cover and simmer 40 minutes or until lentils are tender, stirring occasionally.

Yields: 4 servings.

My Notes

Notes

Notes

Notes

Notes

Notes

Notes

Notes

Notes

Notes

Acknowledgements

The author would like to acknowledge all those individuals who helped me during my time in writing this book. Appreciation is extended for all their support and effort they put into this project.

Deep gratitude and profound thanks are owed to my husband, Jim, for giving freely of his time and encouragement during this project.

Thanks are also owed to my children Gabriel, Brianne Kristina and her husband Moulik Vinodkumar Kothari, Marissa Kimberly and her husband Kevin Matthew Franck, Janelle Karina and her husband Paul Joseph Turcotte, Mikayla Karlene, Kyler James, Kelsey Katrina, Corbin Joel, Caleb Jerome, Keisha Kalani Hiwot, Devontay Joshua, Kianna Karielle Selam, Rosy Kiara, Mercedes Katherine, Jasmine Khalia Wengel, Cheyenne Krystal, and Annalise Kaylee Marie. All of these persons inspired my writing.

Thanks are due to Pam Alexandrovich and Sharron Thompson for their assistance in typing and editing this manuscript for publication. Thanks go to Artistic Design Service, Inc. for their assistance in formatting and providing a graphic design of this manuscript for publication. This project could not have been completed without them.

Many thanks are due to members of my family, all of whom were extremely supportive during the time it took to complete this project. Their patience and support are greatly appreciated.

Current and Future Cookbooks
By Karen Jean Matsko Hood

DELIGHTS SERIES

Almond Delights
Anchovy Delights
Apple Delights
Apricot Delights
Artichoke Delights
Asparagus Delights
Avocado Delights
Banana Delights
Barley Delights
Basil Delights
Bean Delights
Beef Delights
Beer Delights
Beet Delights
Blackberry Delights
Blueberry Delights
Bok Choy Delights
Boysenberry Delights
Brazil Nut Delights
Broccoli Delights
Brussels Sprouts Delights
Buffalo Berry Delights
Butter Delights
Buttermilk Delights
Cabbage Delights
Calamari Delights
Cantaloupe Delights
Caper Delights
Cardamom Delights
Carrot Delights
Cashew Delights
Cauliflower Delights
Celery Delights
Cheese Delights
Cherry Delights
Chestnut Delights
Chicken Delights
Chili Pepper Delights
Chive Delights

Chocolate Delights
Chokecherry Delights
Cilantro Delights
Cinnamon Delights
Clam Delights
Clementine Delights
Coconut Delights
Coffee Delights
Conch Delights
Corn Delights
Cottage Cheese Delights
Crab Delights
Cranberry Delights
Cucumber Delights
Cumin Delights
Curry Delights
Date Delights
Edamame Delights
Egg Delights
Eggplant Delights
Elderberry Delights
Endive Delights
Fennel Delights
Fig Delights
Filbert (Hazelnut) Delights
Fish Delights
Garlic Delights
Ginger Delights
Ginseng Delights
Goji Berry Delights
Grape Delights
Grapefruit Delights
Grapple Delights
Guava Delights
Ham Delights
Hamburger Delights
Herb Delights
Herbal Tea Delights
Honey Delights
Honeyberry Delights
Honeydew Delights

Horseradish Delights
Huckleberry Delights
Jalapeño Delights
Jerusalem Artichoke Delights
Jicama Delights
Kale Delights
Kiwi Delights
Kohlrabi Delights
Lavender Delights
Leek Delights
Lemon Delights
Lentil Delights
Lettuce Delights
Lime Delights
Lingonberry Delights
Lobster Delights
Loganberry Delights
Macadamia Nut Delights
Mango Delights
Marionberry Delights
Milk Delights
Mint Delights
Miso Delights
Mushroom Delights
Mussel Delights
Nectarine Delights
Oatmeal Delights
Olive Delights
Onion Delights
Orange Delights
Oregon Berry Delights
Oyster Delights
Papaya Delights
Parsley Delights
Parsnip Delights
Pea Delights
Peach Delights
Peanut Delights
Pear Delights
Pecan Delights
Pepper Delights
Persimmon Delights
Pine Nut Delights
Pineapple Delights

Pistachio Delights
Plum Delights
Pomegranate Delights
Pomelo Delights
Popcorn Delights
Poppy Seed Delights
Pork Delights
Potato Delights
Prickly Pear Cactus Delights
Prune Delights
Pumpkin Delights
Quince Delights
Quinoa Delights
Radish Delights
Raisin Delights
Raspberry Delights
Rhubarb Delights
Rice Delights
Rose Delights
Rosemary Delights
Rutabaga Delights
Salmon Delights
Salmonberry Delights
Salsify Delights
Savory Delights
Scallop Delights
Seaweed Delights
Serviceberry Delights
Sesame Delights
Shallot Delights
Shrimp Delights
Soybean Delights
Spinach Delights
Squash Delights
Star Fruit Delights
Strawberry Delights
Sunflower Seed Delights
Sweet Potato Delights
Swiss Chard Delights
Tangerine Delights
Tapioca Delights
Tayberry Delights
Tea Delights
Teaberry Delights

Thimbleberry Delights
Tofu Delights
Tomatillo Delights
Tomato Delights
Trout Delights
Truffle Delights
Tuna Delights
Turkey Delights
Turmeric Delights
Turnip Delights
Vanilla Delights
Walnut Delights
Wasabi Delights
Watermelon Delights
Wheat Delights
Wild Rice Delights
Yam Delights
Yogurt Delights
Zucchini Delights

CITY DELIGHTS
Chicago Delights
Coeur d'Alene Delights
Great Falls Delights
Honolulu Delights
Minneapolis Delights
Phoenix Delights
Portland Delights
Sandpoint Delights
Scottsdale Delights
Seattle Delights
Spokane Delights
St. Cloud Delights

FOSTER CARE
Foster Children Cookbook
 and Activity Book
Foster Children's Favorite
 Recipes
Holiday Cookbook for
 Foster Families

GENERAL THEME
 DELIGHTS
Appetizer Delights

Baby Food Delights
Barbeque Delights
Beer-Making Delights
Beverage Delights
Biscotti Delights
Bisque Delights
Blender Delights
Bread Delights
Bread Maker Delights
Breakfast Delights
Brunch Delights
Cake Delights
Campfire Food Delights
Candy Delights
Canned Food Delights
Cast Iron Delights
Cheesecake Delights
Chili Delights
Chowder Delights
Cocktail Delights
College Cooking Delights
Comfort Food Delights
Cookie Delights
Cooking for One Delights
Cooking for Two Delights
Cracker Delights
Crepe Delights
Crockpot Delights
Dairy Delights
Dehydrated Food Delights
Dessert Delights
Dinner Delights
Dutch Oven Delights
Foil Delights
Fondue Delights
Food Processor Delights
Fried Food Delights
Frozen Food Delights
Fruit Delights
Gelatin Delights
Grilled Delights
Hiking Food Delights
Ice Cream Delights
Juice Delights

Kid's Delights
Kosher Diet Delights
Liqueur-Making Delights
Liqueurs and Spirits Delights
Lunch Delights
Marinade Delights
Microwave Delights
Milk Shake and Malt Delights
Panini Delights
Pasta Delights
Pesto Delights
Phyllo Delights
Pickled Food Delights
Picnic Food Delights
Pizza Delights
Preserved Delights
Pudding and Custard Delights
Quiche Delights
Quick Mix Delights
Rainbow Delights
Salad Delights
Salsa Delights
Sandwich Delights
Sea Vegetable Delights
Seafood Delights
Smoothie Delights
Snack Delights
Soup Delights
Supper Delights
Tart Delights
Torte Delights
Tropical Delights
Vegan Delights
Vegetable Delights
Vegetarian Delights
Vinegar Delights
Wildflower Delights
Wine Delights
Winemaking Delights
Wok Delights

GIFTS-IN-A-JAR COOKBOOK SERIES

Christmas Gifts-in-a-Jar –
 Book 1

Gifts-in-a-Jar – Book 2
Holiday Gifts-in-a-Jar –
 Book 3

HEALTH-RELATED DELIGHTS

Achalasia Diet Delights
Adrenal Health Diet Delights
Anti-Acid Reflux Diet Delights
Anti-Cancer Diet Delights
Anti-Inflammation Diet
 Delights
Anti-Stress Diet Delights
Arthritis Delights
Bone Health Diet Delights
Diabetic Diet Delights
Diet for Pink Delights
Fibromyalgia Diet Delights
Gluten-Free Diet Delights
Healthy Breath Diet Delights
Healthy Digestion Diet
 Delights
Healthy Heart Diet Delights
Healthy Skin Diet Delights
Healthy Teeth Diet Delights
High-Fiber Diet Delights
High-Iodine Diet Delights
High-Protein Diet Delights
Immune Health Diet Delights
Kidney Health Diet Delights
Lactose-Free Diet Delights
Liquid Diet Delights
Liver Health Diet Delights
Low-Calorie Diet Delights
Low-Carb Diet Delights
Low-Fat Diet Delights
Low-Sodium Diet Delights
Low-Sugar Diet Delights
Lymphoma Health Support
 Diet Delights
Multiple Sclerosis Healthy
 Diet Delights
No Flour No Sugar Diet
 Delights

Organic Food Delights
pH-Friendly Diet Delights
Pregnancy Diet Delights
Raw Food Diet Delights
Sjögren's Syndrome Diet
 Delights
Soft Food Diet Delights
Thyroid Health Diet Delights

HOLIDAY DELIGHTS
Christmas Delights
Easter Delights
Father's Day Delights
Fourth of July Delights
Grandparent's Day Delights
Halloween Delights
Hanukkah Delights
Labor Day Delights
Memorial Day Delights
Mother's Day Delights
New Year's Delights
St. Patrick's Day Delights
Thanksgiving Delights
Valentine Delights

HOOD AND MATSKO
FAMILY FAVORITES
Hood and Matsko Family
 Appetizers Cookbook
Hood and Matsko Family
 Beverages Cookbook
Hood and Matsko Family
 Breads and Rolls Cookbook
Hood and Matsko Family
 Breakfasts Cookbook
Hood and Matsko Family
 Cakes Cookbook
Hood and Matsko Family
 Candies Cookbook
Hood and Matsko Family
 Casseroles Cookbook
Hood and Matsko Family
 Cookies Cookbook
Hood and Matsko Family

Desserts Cookbook
Hood and Matsko Family
 Dressings, Sauces, and
 Condiments Cookbook
Hood and Matsko Family
 Ethnic Cookbook
Hood and Matsko Family
 Jams, Jellies, Syrups,
 Preserves, and Conserves
Hood and Matsko Family
 Main Dishes Cookbook
Hood and Matsko Family,
 Pies Cookbook
Hood and Matsko Family
 Preserving Cookbook
Hood and Matsko Family
 Salads and Salad Dressings
Hood and Matsko Family
 Side Dishes Cookbook
Hood and Matsko Family
 Vegetable Cookbook
Hood and Matsko Family,
 Aunt Katherine's Recipe
 Collection, Vol. I-II
Hood and Matsko Family,
 Grandma Bert's Recipe
 Collection, Books 1-8

HOOD AND MATSKO
FAMILY HOLIDAY
Hood and Matsko Family
 Favorite Birthday Recipes
Hood and Matsko Family
 Favorite Christmas Recipes
Hood and Matsko Family
 Favorite Christmas Sweets
Hood and Matsko Family
 Easter Cookbook
Hood and Matsko Family
 Favorite Thanksgiving Recipes

INTERNATIONAL
DELIGHTS
African Delights

African American Delights
Australian Delights
Austrian Delights
Brazilian Delights
Canadian Delights
Chilean Delights
Chinese Delights
Czechoslovakian Delights
English Delights
Ethiopian Delights
Fijian Delights
French Delights
German Delights
Greek Delights
Hungarian Delights
Icelandic Delights
Indian Delights
Irish Delights
Italian Delights
Korean Delights
Kosovo Delights
Macedonia Republic Delights
Mexican Delights
Montenegro Delights
Native American Delights
Polish Delights
Russian Delights
Scottish Delights
Serbian Delights
Slovakian Delights
Slovenian Delights
Sri Lanka Delights
Swedish Delights
Thai Delights
The Netherlands Delights
Yugoslavian Delights
Zambian Delights

REGIONAL DELIGHTS
Glacier National Park Delights
Northwest Regional Delights
Oregon Coast Delights
Schweitzer Mountain Delights
Southwest Regional Delights
Tropical Delights

Washington Wine Country
 Delights
Wine Delights of Walla
 Walla Wineries
Yellowstone National Park
 Delights

SEASONAL DELIGHTS
Autumn Harvest Delights
Spring Harvest Delights
Summer Harvest Delights
Winter Harvest Delights

SPECIAL EVENTS
 DELIGHTS
Birthday Delights
Coffee Klatch Delights
Super Bowl Delights
Tea Time Delights

STATE DELIGHTS
Alaska Delights
Arizona Delights
Georgia Delights
Hawaii Delights
Idaho Delights
Illinois Delights
Iowa Delights
Louisiana Delights
Minnesota Delights
Montana Delights
North Dakota Delights
Oregon Delights
South Dakota Delights
Texas Delights
Washington Delights

U.S. TERRITORIES
 DELIGHTS
Cruzan Delights
U.S. Virgin Island Delights

MISCELLANEOUS
 COOKBOOKS
Getaway Studio Cookbook
The Soup Doctor's Cookbook

BILINGUAL DELIGHTS SERIES

Apple Delights, English-French Edition
Apple Delights, English-Russian Edition
Apple Delights, English-Spanish Edition
Huckleberry Delights, English-French Edition
Huckleberry Delight`s, English-Russian Edition
Huckleberry Delights, English-Spanish Edition

CATHOLIC DELIGHTS SERIES

Apple Delights Catholic
Coffee Delights Catholic
Easter Delights Catholic
Huckleberry Delights Catholic
Tea Delights Catholic

CATHOLIC BILINGUAL DELIGHTS SERIES

Apple Delights Catholic, English-French Edition
Apple Delights Catholic, English-Russian Edition
Apple Delights Catholic, English-Spanish Edition
Huckleberry Delights Catholic, English-Spanish Edition

CHRISTIAN DELIGHTS SERIES

Apple Delights Christian
Coffee Delights Christian
Easter Delights Christian
Huckleberry Delights Christian
Tea Delights Christian

CHRISTIAN BILINGUAL DELIGHTS SERIES

Apple Delights Christian, English-French Edition
Apple Delights Christian, English-Russian Edition
Apple Delights Christian, English-Spanish Edition
Huckleberry Delights Christian, English-Spanish Edition

FUNDRAISING COOKBOOKS

Ask about our fundraising cookbooks to help raise funds for your organization.

The above books are also available in bilingual versions. Please contact Whispering Pine Press International, Inc., for details.
The above list of books is not all-inclusive. For a complete list please visit our website or contact us at:

Whispering Pine Press International, Inc.
Your Northwest Book Publishing Company
2510 North Pines Road, Suite 206, Sales Room
Spokane Valley, WA 99206-7636 USA
Phone: (509) 928-7888 | Fax: (509) 922-9949
Email: sales@whisperingpinepress.com
Publisher Websites: www.WhisperingPinePress.com www.WhisperingPinePressBookstore.com
Blog: www.WhisperingPinePressBlog.com

Publisher Websites:
Main Website: WhisperingPinePress.com
Online Store: WhisperingPinePressBookstore.com
WordPress Blogs: WhisperingPinePressBlog.com
WhisperingPinePressKidsBooks.com
WhisperingPinePressTeenBooks.com
WhisperingPinePressPoetry.com

Karen Jean Matsko Hood
Author Website: KarenJeanMatskoHood.com
Online Store: KarenJeanMatskoHoodBookstore.com
Author Blog: KarenJeanMatskoHoodBlog.com
Kids Books: KarensKidsBooks.com
Teen Books: KarensTeenBooks.com

Author's Social Media
Like or Friend the Author on Facebook:
https://www.facebook.com/KarenJeanMatskoHoodAuthor
FanPage
Follow the Author on Twitter:
https://twitter.com/KarenJeanHood
Google Plus Profile:
http://google.com/+KarenJeanMatskoHood

G l o s s a r y

Aerate: A synonym for sift; to pass ingredients through a fine-mesh device to break up large pieces and incorporate air into ingredients to make them lighter.

Al dente: "To the tooth," in Italian. The pasta is cooked just enough to maintain a firm, chewy texture.

Baste: To brush or spoon liquid fat or juices over meat during roasting to add flavor and prevent it from drying out.

Bias-slice: To slice a food crosswise at a 45-degree angle.

Bind: To thicken a sauce or hot liquid by stirring in ingredients such as eggs, flour, butter, or cream.

Blackened: Popular Cajun-style cooking method.Seasoned foods are cooked over high heat in a super-heated heavy skillet until charred.

Blanch: To boil briefly to loosen the skin of a fruit or a vegetable. After 30 seconds in boiling water, the fruit or vegetable should be plunged into ice water to stop the cooking action, and then the skin easily peels off.

Blend: To mix or fold two or more ingredients together to obtain equal distribution throughout the mixture.

*Braise:*A cooking technique that requires browning meat in oil or other fat and then cooking slowly in liquid. The effect of braising is to tenderize the meat.

Bread: To coat the food with crumbs (usually with soft or dry bread crumbs), sometimes seasoned.

Brown: A quick sautéing, pan/oven broiling, or grilling method done either at the beginning or end of meal preparation, often to enhance flavor, texture, or eye appeal.

Brush: Using a pastry brush, to coat a food such as meat or bread with melted butter, glaze, or other liquid.

Bundt pan: The generic name for any tube baking pan having fluted sides (though it was once a trademarked name).

Butterfly: To cut open a food such as pork chops down the center without cutting all the way through, and then spread apart.

Caramelization: Browning sugar over a flame, with or without the addition of some water to aid the process. The temperature range in which sugar caramelizes is approximately 320º F to 360º F (160º C to 182º C).

Clarify: Remove impurities from butter or stock by heating the liquid, then straining or skimming it.

Coddle: A cooking method in which foods (such as eggs) are put in separate containers and placed in a pan of simmering water for slow, gentle cooking.

Confit: To slowly cook pieces of meat in their own gently rendered fat.

Core: To remove the inedible center of fruits such as pineapples.

Cream: To beat vegetable shortening, butter, or margarine, with or without sugar, until light and fluffy. This process traps in air bubbles, later used to create height in cookies and cakes.

Crimp: To create a decorative edge on a piecrust. On a double piecrust, this also seals the edges together.

Curd: Custard-like pie or tart filling flavored with juice and zest of citrus fruit, usually lemon, although lime and orange may also be used.

Curdle: To cause semisolid pieces of coagulated protein to develop in food, usually as a result of the addition of an acid substance, or the overheating of milk or egg-based sauces.

Custard: A mixture of beaten egg, milk, and possibly other ingredients such as sweet or savory flavorings, which is cooked with gentle heat, often in a water bath or double boiler. As pie filling, the custard is frequently cooked and chilled before being layered into a baked crust.

Deglaze: To add liquid to a pan in which foods have been fried or roasted, in order to dissolve the caramelized juices stuck to the bottom of the pan.

Dot: To sprinkle food with small bits of an ingredient such as butter to allow for even melting.

Dredge: To sprinkle lightly and evenly with sugar or flour. A dredger has holes pierced on the lid to sprinkle evenly.

Drizzle: To pour a liquid such as a sweet glaze or melted butter in a slow, light trickle over food.

Drippings: Used for gravies and sauces, drippings are the liquids left in the bottom of a roasting or frying pan after meat is cooked.

Dust: To sprinkle food lightly with spices, sugar, or flour for a light coating.

Egg wash: A mixture of beaten eggs (yolks, whites, or whole eggs) with either milk or water. Used to coat cookies and other baked goods to give them a shine when baked.

Emulsion: A mixture of liquids, one being a fat or oil and the other being water based so that tiny globules of one are suspended in the other. This may involve the use of stabilizers, such as egg or mustard. Emulsions may be temporary or permanent.

Entrée: A French term that originally referred to the first course of a meal, served after the soup and before the meat courses. In the United States, it refers to the main dish of a meal.

Fillet: To remove the bones from meat or fish for cooking.

Filter: To remove lumps, excess liquid, or impurities by passing through paper or cheesecloth.

Firm-ball stage: In candy making, the point where boiling syrup dropped in cold water forms a ball that is compact yet gives slightly to the touch.

Flambé: To ignite a sauce or other liquid so that it flames.

Flan: An open pie filled with sweet or savory ingredients; also, a Spanish dessert of baked custard covered with caramel.

Flute: To create a decorative scalloped or undulating edge on a piecrust or other pastry.

Fricassee: Usually a stew in which the meat is cut up, lightly cooked in butter, and then simmered in liquid until done.

Frizzle: To cook thin slices of meat in hot oil until crisp and slightly curly.

Ganache: A rich chocolate filling or coating made with chocolate, vegetable shortening, and possibly heavy cream. It can coat cakes or cookies, and be used as a filling for truffles.

Glaze: A liquid that gives an item a shiny surface. Examples are fruit jams that have been heated or chocolate thinned with melted vegetable shortening. Also, to cover a food with such a liquid.

Gratin: To bind together or combine food with a liquid such as cream, milk, béchamel sauce, or tomato sauce, in a shallow dish. The mixture is then baked until cooked and set.

Hard-ball stage: In candy making, the point at which syrup has cooked long enough to form a solid ball in cold water.

Hull (also husk): To remove the leafy parts of soft fruits, such as strawberries or blackberries.

Infusion: Extracting flavors by soaking them in liquid heated in a covered pan. The term also refers to the liquid resulting from this process.

Jerk or Jamaican jerk seasoning: A dry mixture of various spices such as chilies, thyme, garlic, onions, and cinnamon or cloves used to season meats such as chicken or pork.

Julienne: To cut into long, thin strips.

Jus: The natural juices released by roasting meats.

Larding: Inserting strips of fat into pieces of meat, so that the braised meat stays moist and juicy.

Marble: To gently swirl one food into another.

Marinate: To combine food with aromatic ingredients to add flavor.

Meringue: Egg whites beaten until they are stiff, then sweetened. It can be used as the topping for pies, or baked as cookies.

Mull: To slowly heat wine or cider with spices and sugar.

Parboil: To partly cook in a boiling liquid.

Peaks: The mounds made in a mixture. For example, egg white that has been whipped to stiffness. Peaks are "stiff" if they stay upright, or "soft" if they curl over.

Pesto: A sauce usually made of fresh basil, garlic, olive oil, pine nuts, and cheese. The ingredients are finely chopped and then mixed, uncooked, with pasta. Generally, the term refers to any uncooked sauce made of finely chopped herbs and nuts.

Pipe: To force a semi-soft food through a bag (either a pastry bag or a plastic bag with one corner cut off) to decorate food.

Pressure Cooking: A cooking method that uses steam trapped under a locked lid to produce high temperatures and achieve fast cooking time.

Ramekin: A small baking dish used for individual servings of sweet and savory dishes.

Reduce: To cook liquids down so that some of the water evaporates.

Refresh: To pour cold water over freshly cooked vegetables to prevent further cooking and to retain color.

Roux: A cooked paste usually made from flour and butter used to thicken sauces.

Sauté: To cook food quickly in a small amount of oil in a skillet or sauté pan over direct heat.

Sear: Sealing in a meat's juices by cooking it quickly under very high heat.

Seize: To form a thick, lumpy mass when melted (usually applied to chocolate).

Sift: To remove large lumps from a dry ingredient such as flour or confectioners' sugar by passing it through a fine mesh. This process also incorporates air into the ingredients, making them lighter.

Simmer: Cooking food in a liquid at a low enough temperature that small bubbles begin to break the surface.

Steam: To cook over boiling water in a covered pan, this method keeps foods' shape, texture, and nutritional value intact better than methods such as boiling.

Steep: To soak dry ingredients (tea leaves, ground coffee, herbs, spices, etc.) in liquid until the flavor is infused into the liquid.

Stewing: Browning small pieces of meat, poultry, or fish, then simmering them with vegetables or other ingredients in enough liquid to cover them, usually in a closed pot on the stove, in the oven, or with a slow cooker.

Thin: To reduce a mixture's thickness with the addition of more liquid.

Truss: To use string, skewers, or pins to hold together a food to maintain its shape while it cooks (usually applied to meat or poultry).

Unleavened: Baked goods that contain no agents to give them volume, such as baking powder, baking soda, or yeast.

Vinaigrette: A general term referring to any sauce made with vinegar, oil, and seasonings.

Zest: The thin, brightly colored outer part of the rind of citrus fruits. It contains volatile oils, used as a flavoring.

U.S. and Metric Measurement Charts

Here are some measurement equivalents to help you with exchanges. There was a time when many people thought the entire world would convert to the metric scale. While most of the world has, America still has not. Metric conversions in cooking are vitally important to preparing a tasty recipe. Here are simple conversion tables that should come in handy.

U.S. Measurement Equivalents

a few grains/pinch/dash (dry) = less than ⅛ teaspoon
a dash (liquid) = a few drops
3 teaspoons = 1 tablespoon
½ tablespoon = 1½ teaspoons
1 tablespoon = 3 teaspoons
2 tablespoons = 1 fluid ounce
4 tablespoons = ¼ cup
5⅓ tablespoons = ⅓ cup
8 tablespoons = ½ cup
8 tablespoons = 4 fluid ounces
10⅔ tablespoons = ⅔ cup
12 tablespoons = ¾ cup
16 tablespoons = 1 cup
16 tablespoons = 8 fluid ounces
⅛ cup = 2 tablespoons
¼ cup = 4 tablespoons
¼ cup = 2 fluid ounces
⅓ cup = 5 tablespoons plus 1 teaspoon
½ cup = 8 tablespoons
1 cup = 16 tablespoons
1 cup = 8 fluid ounces
1 cup = ½ pint
2 cups = 1 pint
2 pints = 1 quart
4 quarts (liquid) = 1 gallon
8 quarts (dry) = 1 peck
4 pecks (dry) = 1 bushel
1 kilogram = approximately 2 pounds
1 liter=approximately 4 cups or 1quart

Approximate Metric Equivalents by Volume

U.S. Metric
¼ cup = 60 milliliters
½ cup = 120 milliliters
1 cup = 230 milliliters
1¼ cups = 300 milliliters
1½ cups = 360 milliliters
2 cups = 460 milliliters
2½ cups = 600 milliliters
3 cups = 700 milliliters
4 cups (1 quart) = .95 liter
1.06 quarts = 1 liter
4 quarts (1 gallon) = 3.8 liters

Approximate Metric Equivalents by Weight

U.S. Metric
¼ ounce = 7 grams
½ ounce = 14 grams
1 ounce = 28 grams
1¼ ounces = 35 grams
1½ ounces = 40 grams
2½ ounces = 70 grams
4 ounces = 112 grams
5 ounces = 140 grams
8 ounces = 228 grams
10 ounces = 280 grams
15 ounces = 425 grams
16 ounces (1 pound) = 454 grams

Holiday Gifts-in-a-Jar Cookbook Index

Scones

Seasonings

Side Dishes

Soups

Reader Feedback Form

Dear Reader,

    We are very interested in what our readers think. Please fill in the form below and return to:

Whispering Pine Press International, Inc.
c/o Holiday Gifts-in-a-Jar Cookbook
2510 North Pines Road, Suite 206, Sales Room
Spokane Valley, WA 99206-7636 USA
Phone: (509) 928-7888 | Fax: (509) 922-9949
Email: sales@whisperingpinepress.com
Website: www.WhisperingPinePress.com
www.WhisperingPinePressBookstore.com
Blog: www.WhisperingPinePressBlog.com
SANS #253-200X

Name: _____

Address: _____

City, St., Zip: _____

Phone/Fax: (____) _____ | (____) _____

Email: _____

Comments/Suggestions: _____

_____

_____

_____

_____

    A great deal of care and attention has been exercised in the creation of this book. Designing a great cookbook that is original, fun, and easy to use has been a job that required many hours of diligence, creativity, and research. Although we strive to make this book completely error free, errors and discrepancies may not be completely excluded. If you come across any errors or discrepancies, please make a note of them and send them to our publishing office. We are constantly updating our manuscripts, eliminating errors, and improving quality.

Please contact us at the address above.

About the Gifts-in-a-Jar Series

The *Gifts-in-a-Jar Cookbook Series* includes many different recipes that are fun and easy to make. If you have a passion for food and wish to make some great gifts to share with friends and family, then this series of cookbooks will be beneficial to you.

Gifts-in-a-Jar Cookbook Series includes Christmas Gifts-in-a-Jar, Gifts-in-a-Jar, and Holiday Gifts-in-a-Jar. Each book features different types of recipes for Gifts-in-a-Jar.

Whatever your favorite holiday may be, chances are we have a cookbook with recipes designed with that holiday in mind. Some examples include *Valentine Delights, St. Patrick's Day Delights, Easter Delights, Mother's Day Delights, Halloween Delights, Thanksgiving Delights, and Christmas Delights.*

Each cookbook is designed for easy use and is organized into alphabetical sections. Each book comes with a beautiful full-color cover, ordering information, and a list of other upcoming books in the series.

Note cards, bookmarks, and a daily journal have been printed and are available to go along with each cookbook. You may view the entire line of cookbooks, journals, cards, posters, puzzles, and bookmarks by visiting our website at www.WhisperingPinePressBookstore.com, or you can email us with your questions and your comments to: sales@whisperingpinepress.com.

Please ask your local bookstore to carry these sets of books.

To order, please contact:

Whispering Pine Press International, Inc.
c/o Holiday Gifts-in-a-Jar Cookbook
2510 North Pines Road, Suite 206, Sales Room
Spokane Valley, WA 99206-7636 USA
Phone: (509) 928-7888 | Fax: (509) 922-9949
Email: sales@whisperingpinepress.com
Publisher Websites: www.WhisperingPinePress.com
www.WhisperingPinePressBookstore.com
Blog: www.WhisperingPinePressBlog.com
SAN 253-200X

We Invite You to Join the Whispering Pine Press International, Inc. Book Club!

Whispering Pine Press International, Inc.
c/o Holiday Gifts-in-a-Jar Cookbook
2510 North Pines Road, Suite 206, Sales Room
Spokane Valley, WA 99206-7636 USA
Phone: (509) 928-7888 | Fax: (509) 922-9949
Email: sales@whisperingpinepress.com
Publisher Websites: www.WhisperingPinePress.com
www.WhisperingPinePressBookstore.com
Blog: www.WhisperingPinePressBlog.com

Buy 11 books and get the next one free, based on the average price of the first eleven purchased.

How the club works:

Simply use the order form below and order books from our catalog. You can buy just one at a time or all eleven at once. After the first eleven books are purchased, the next one is free. Please add shipping and handling as listed on this form. There are no purchase requirements at any time during your membership. Free book credit is based on the average price of the first eleven books purchased.

Join today! Pick your books and mail in the form today!

Yes! I want to join the Whispering Pine Press International, Inc., Book Club! Enroll me and send the books indicated below.

Title   Price

1. _____

2. _____

3. _____

4. _____

5. _____

6. _____

7. _____

8. _____

9. _____

10. _____

11. _____

Free Book Title: _____

Free Book Price: _____ Avg. Price: _____ Total Price: _____

Credit for the free book is based on the average price of the first 11 books purchased.

(Circle one) Check|Visa|MasterCard|Discover|American Express

Credit Card #: _____ Expiration Date: _____

Name: _____

Address: _____

City: _____State: _____Country: _____

Zip/Postal: _____Phone: (_____) _____

Email: _____

Signature _____

Whispering Pine Press International, Inc. Fundraising Opportunities

Fundraising cookbooks are proven moneymakers and great keepsake providers for your group. Whispering Pine Press International, Inc., offers a very special personalized cookbook fundraising program that encourages success to organizations all across the USA.

Our prices are competitive and fair. Currently, we offer a special of 100 books with many free features and excellent customer service. Any purchase you make is guaranteed first-rate.

Flexibility is not a problem. If you have special needs, we guarantee our cooperation in meeting each of them. Our goal is to create a cookbook that goes beyond your expectations. We have the confidence and a record that promises continual success.

Another great fundraising program is the *Cookbook Delights Series* Program. With cookbook orders of 50 copies or more, your organization receives a huge discount, making for a prompt and lucrative solution.

We also specialize in assisting group fundraising – Christian, community, nonprofit, and academic among them. If you are struggling for a new idea, something that will enhance your success and broaden your appeal, Whispering Pine Press International, Inc., can help.

For more information, write, phone, or fax to:

Whispering Pine Press International, Inc.
2510 North Pines Road, Suite 206, Sales Room
Spokane Valley, WA 99206-7636 USA
Phone: (509) 928-7888 | Fax: (509) 922-9949
Email: sales@whisperingpinepress.com
Publisher Websites: www.WhisperingPinePress.com
www.WhisperingPinePressBookstore.com
Blog: www.WhisperingPinePressBlog.com
Book Website: www.GiftsInJars.com
SAN 253-200X

Personalized and/or Translated
Order Form for Any Book by
Whispering Pine Press International, Inc.

Dear Readers:

If you or your organization wishes to have this book or any other of our books personalized, we will gladly accommodate your needs. For instance, if you would like to change the names of the characters in a book to the names of the children in your family or Sunday school class, we would be happy to work with you on such a project. We can add more information of your choosing and customize this book especially for your family, group, or organization.

We are also offering an option of translating your book into another language. Please fill out the form below telling us exactly how you would like us to personalize your book.

Please send your request to:

Whispering Pine Press International, Inc.
c/o Holiday Gifts-in-a-Jar Cookbook
2510 North Pines Road, Suite 206, Sales Room
Spokane Valley, WA 99206-7636 USA
Phone: (509) 928-7888 | Fax: (509) 922-9949
Email: sales@whisperingpinepress.com
Publisher Websites: www.WhisperingPinePress.com
www.WhisperingPinePressBookstore.com
Blog: www.WhisperingPinePressBlog.com

Person/Organization placing request: _____

Date_____ Phone: (____)_____

Address_____ Fax: (____)_____

City_____ State_____ Zip: _____

Language of the book: _____

Please explain your request in detail: _____

_____

_____

_____

_____

_____

Holiday Gifts-in-a-Jar Cookbook
A Collection of Holiday Gifts-in-a-Jar Recipes

How to Order

Get your additional copies of this book by returning an order form and your check, money order, or credit card information to:

Whispering Pine Press International, Inc.
c/o Holiday Gifts-in-a-Jar Cookbook
2510 North Pines Road, Suite 206, Sales Room
Spokane Valley, WA 99206-7636 USA
Phone: (509) 928-7888 | Fax: (509) 922-9949
Email: sales@whisperingpinepress.com
Publisher Websites: www.WhisperingPinePress.com
www.WhisperingPinePressBookstore.com
Blog: www.WhisperingPinePressBlog.com

Customer Name: _____

Address: _____

City, St., Zip: _____

Phone/Fax: _____

Email: _____

- -

Please send me _____ copies of _____ _____

_____ at $_____ per copy and $5.95 for shipping and handling per book, plus $3.95 each for additional books. Enclosed is my check, money order, or charge my account for $_____.

☐ Check ☐ Money Order ☐ Credit Card

(*Circle One*) MasterCard | Discover | Visa | American Express

☐☐☐☐ ☐☐☐☐ ☐☐☐☐ ☐☐☐☐

Expiration Date: _____

_____
Signature

_____
Print Name

Whispering Pine Press International, Inc. Order Form

Gift-wrapping, Autographing, and Inscription
We are proud to offer personal autographing by the author. For a limited time this service is absolutely free!
Gift-wrapping is also available for $4.95 per item.

1. Sold To
Name: _____
Street/Route: _____
_____
City: _____
State: _____ Zip: _____
Country: _____
Gift message: _____
_____
Email address: _____
Daytime Phone: (_ _ _) _ _ _-_ _ _ _
*Necessary for verifying orders
Home Phone: (_ _ _) _ _ _-_ _ _ _
Fax: (_ _ _) _ _ _-_ _ _ _

2. Ship To
☐ Is this a new or corrected address?

☐ Alternative Shipping Address

☐ Mailing Address
Name: _____
Address: _____
_____
City: _____
State: _____ Zip: _____
Country: _____
Email address: _____

3. Items Ordered

ISBN # /Item #	Size	Color	Qty.	Title or Description	Price	Total

4. Method Of Payment
International, Inc. (No Cash or COD's)

☐ Visa ☐ MasterCard ☐ Discover ☐ American Express ☐ Check/Money Order
Please make it payable to Whispering Pine Press International, Inc. (No Cash or COD's)

Account Number   Expiration Date
_____ / _____
Month Year

☐☐☐☐☐☐☐☐☐☐☐☐☐☐☐☐

Signature_____
Cardholder's signature

Printed Name_____
Please print name of cardholder
Address of Cardholder_____

Subtotal	
Gift wrap $4.95 Each	
For delivery in WA add 8.7% sales tax.	
Shipping See chart at left	
6. Total	

5. Shipping & Handling

Continental US
US Postal Ground: For books please add $4.95 for the first book and $2.95 each for additional books.
All non-book items, add 15% of the Subtotal.
Please allow 1-4 weeks for delivery.
US Postal Air: Please add $15.00 shipping and handling.
Please allow 1-3 days for delivery.
Alaska, Hawaii, and the US Territories By Ship:
Please add 10% shipping and handling (minimum charge $15.00).

Please
By Air: Please add 12% shipping and handling (minimum charge $15.00).
Please allow 2 –6 weeks for delivery.
International By Ship: Please add 10% shipping and handling (minimum charge $15.00).
Please allow 6-12 weeks for delivery.
By Air: Please add 12% shipping and handling (minimum charge $15.00).
Please allow 2-6 weeks for delivery.
FedEx Shipments: Add $5.00 to the above airmail charges for overnight delivery.

Shop Online:
www.WhisperingPinePress.com
Fax orders to: (509) 922-9949

Whispering Pine Press International, Inc.
2510 North Pines Road, Suite 206, Sales Room
Spokane Valley, WA 99206-7636 USA
Phone: (509) 928-7888 • Fax: (509) 922-9949
Email: sales@whisperingpinepress.com
Website: www.WhisperingPinePress.com

About the Author and Cook

Karen Jean Matsko Hood has always enjoyed cooking, baking, and experimenting with recipes. At this time Hood is working to complete a series of cookbooks that blends her skills and experience in cooking and entertaining. Hood entertains large groups of people and especially enjoys designing creative menus with holiday, international, ethnic, and regional themes.

Hood is publishing a cookbook series entitled the *Cookbook Delights Series*, in which each cookbook emphasizes a different food ingredient or theme. The first cookbook in the series is *Apple Delights Cookbook*. Hood is working to complete another series of cookbooks titled *Hood and Matsko Family Cookbooks*, which includes many recipes handed down from her family heritage and others that have emerged from more current family traditions. She has been invited to speak on talk radio shows on various topics, and favorite recipes from her cookbooks have been prepared on local television programs.

Hood was born and raised in Great Falls, Montana. As an undergraduate, she attended the College of St. Benedict in St. Joseph, Minnesota, and St. John's University in Collegeville, Minnesota. She attended the University of Great Falls in Great Falls, Montana. Hood received a B.S. Degree in Natural Science from the College of St. Benedict and minored in both Psychology and Secondary Education. Upon her graduation, Hood and her husband taught science and math on the island of St. Croix in the U.S. Virgin Islands. Hood has completed postgraduate classes at the University of Iowa in Iowa City, Iowa. In May 2001, she completed her Master's Degree in Pastoral Ministry at Gonzaga University in Spokane, Washington. She has taken postgraduate classes at Lewis and Clark College on the North Idaho college campus in Coeur d'Alene, Idaho, Taylor University in Fort Wayne, Indiana, Spokane Falls Community College, Spokane Community College, Washington State University, University of Washington, and Eastern Washington University. Hood is working on research projects to complete her Ph.D. in Leadership Studies at Gonzaga University in Spokane, Washington.

Hood resides in Spokane, Washington, along with her husband, many of her sixteen children, and foster children. Her interests include writing, research, and teaching. She previously has volunteered as a court advocate in the Spokane juvenile court system for abused and neglected children. Hood is a literary advocate for youth and adults. Her hobbies include cooking, baking, collecting, photography, indoor and outdoor gardening, farming, and the cultivation of unusual flowering plants and orchids. She enjoys raising several specialty breeds of animals including Babydoll Southdown, Friesen Icelandic sheep, Icelandic horses, bichons frisés, cockapoos, Icelandic sheepdogs, a Newfoundland, a Rottweiler, a variety of Nubian and fainting goats and a few rescue cats. Hood also enjoys bird-watching and finds all aspects of nature precious.

She demonstrates a passionate appreciation of the environment and a respect for all life. She also invites you to visit her websites at:

www.KarenJeanMatskoHood.com
www.KarenJeanMatskoHoodBookstore.com
www.KarenJeanMatskoHoodBlog.com
www.Karen'sKidsBooks.com

www.HoodFamilyBlog.com
www.HoodFamily.com

Author's Social Media
Friend her on **Facebook**: Karen Jean Matsko Hood Author Fan Page
Please Follow the Author on **Twitter**: @KarenJeanHood
Google Plus Profile: Karen Jean Matsko Hood
Pinterest.com/KarenJMHood

www.ingramcontent.com/pod-product-compliance
Lightning Source LLC
Chambersburg PA
CBHW070807100426
42742CB00012B/2278